65/

SHARJAH
HERITAGE & PROGRESS

Written and photographed
by Shirley Kay

Published with
the support and
encouragement of the
Government of Sharjah

FOREWORD

In the name of Allah
The Most Beneficent, The Most Merciful

The past quarter of a century has seen Sharjah emerge from Trucial underdevelopment to a thriving metropolis and a modern state of the UAE on the eastern shores of the Arabian Gulf. This transformation was made possible by the discovery of oil and gas in the Emirate, and in other parts of the UAE, coupled with a realistic plan to ensure, as far as practicable, an even development in the various sectors of the national economy.

Research, modern methods of farming and the judicious use of vital available water resources benefited agriculture, while trade, industry and commerce flourished under the Emirate's liberal laws.

The welfare of the people, which has always been paramount, has equally kept pace with other developments. Education, housing, health and other social services were created to meet the demands of the growing nation.

Sharjah, in keeping with its traditional hospitality, has kept open its doors to the international community, attracting vast numbers of trading and professional people, together with tourists who come to enjoy the environmental and modern amenities provided by this flourishing state.

This book highlights the progress in Sharjah to lay down the foundation for a society guided by the tenets of the Islamic faith and in better health and education to be able to take its rightful place among the community of nations in a changing world.

H H Dr Sheikh Sultan bin Mohammed Al Qasimi

His Highness Dr Sheikh Sultan bin Mohammed Al Qasimi
Member of the Supreme Council of the UAE and Ruler of Sharjah

Published by
Motivate Publishing

PO Box 2331
Dubai, UAE
Tel: 246060
Fax: 245270

PO Box 43072
Abu Dhabi, UAE
Tel: 311666
Fax: 311888

London House
26/40, Kensington High Street
London W8 4PF
Tel: 071 937 4024
Fax: 071 937 7293

Directors:
Obaid Humaid Al Tayer
Ian Fairservice

Senior Editor:
Julia Roles

First published 1992

ISBN 1 873544 33 2

Printed by Emirates Printing Press, Dubai

*Cover : The King Faisal Mosque
and Islamic Centre, with the
'New Souq' behind.*

*Contents page: The elegant Souq
Al Majarra on the creekside.*

CONTENTS

SHARJAH AND THE UAE

Sharjah is situated at the heart of the group of seven autonomous Emirates (the other six being Abu Dhabi, Dubai, Ras Al Khaimah, Ajman, Fujairah and Umm Al Quwain) which make up the federation of the United Arab Emirates. For the last 300 years or more Sharjah has been ruled by the Al Qasimi family, who were in the past the greatest Arab maritime power in the Gulf. The present Ruler of Sharjah, HH Dr Sheikh Sultan bin Mohammed Al Qasimi, is the direct descendant of a very long line of Qawasim Sheikhs but the first to gain a PhD from a British university.

The UAE lies at the south-western tip of the Arabian peninsula. It borders the sandy shores of the Gulf's southern coastline, and straddles the rocky interior of the peninsula which runs northwards towards the Strait of Hormuz. In summer this is one of the hottest regions of the world, with temperatures rising above 45°C and humidity reaching 100 per cent at times. Rainfall is scarce, some 10 centimetres a year on average, and the land for the most part is sandy desert or barren rocky mountains. In winter, however, the Emirates enjoys one of the most idyllic climates in the world, with day after day of clear sunshine, comfortable temperatures, and only rare days of rain and cloudy skies. So the country is rapidly becoming one of the world's most recently favoured tourist resorts.

The United Arab Emirates is also one of the world's newer states. It was founded in December 1971, to take the place of the formerly British-protected Trucial States, and was immediately recognised as an independent nation and member of the United Nations. For 150 years Britain had had treaty relations with the individual 'city states'

A typical desert landscape in the Emirate of Sharjah.

High-rise buildings border lush parks in today's Abu Dhabi.

which together constituted the Trucial States. But for most of that time the British interest was purely maritime and it was only in the mid-20th century that British presence onland became more and more pervasive. When the British announced in 1968 that they were to withdraw from east of Suez, the rulers of the individual emirates agreed together to create a united country.

Today this region is one of the richest in the world, and experiencing the most rapid development. But this was not always so. Its intractable desert terrain supported only the most minimal agriculture; its only known exploitable resources were the natural pearls which flourished in the warm waters of the Gulf, and could be collected each summer only by dint of immense effort. Pearls and maritime trade, were thus the major sources of livelihood of the region. The inhabitants of the country were for the most part a tough, desert people who worked hard to maintain a subsistence economy.

Discovery of oil

By the 1950s, however, oil companies were beginning to prospect in this corner of Arabia also. Hopes were high that oil, which had already been discovered in Bahrain, Saudi Arabia, Kuwait and Qatar, might be found here too. So it became necessary to determine ownership of the desert hinterland and the shallow seas. The old informal and fluctuating claims to land ownership would no longer suffice. For the first time in history, formal boundaries were drawn up between one emirate and another.

Palm trees and sand dunes in the Liwa oasis.

In 1959 oil was struck under Abu Dhabi's desert and shortly afterwards it was found under Abu Dhabi's seas as well. The first oil was exported from there in 1962 and was followed by such increasing quantities of oil exports that Abu Dhabi, the most desert-oriented of all the Emirates, was soon to become by far the richest state in the land. Today, Abu Dhabi is estimated to possess enough proven oil reserves to last at present rates of extraction for at least two centuries more! And it enjoys one of the world's highest per capita incomes.

Meanwhile oil was discovered also in Dubai's offshore areas. From there it was first exported in 1969, though nowhere near the quantities that were found in Abu Dhabi. It was enough, however, to provide a welcome boost to Dubai's already active merchant economy, and to bring the start

Camels approach an oil field in Dubai's desert.

9

of prosperity to that Emirate before the independent United Arab Emirates was founded.

Abu Dhabi and Dubai are both ruled by members of the same tribe, the Bani Yas, whose homeland had originally been in the Liwa oasis of southern Abu Dhabi. In Abu Dhabi the ruling branch of the tribe are the Al Nahyan, while in Dubai the Al Maktoum family have ruled for more than a century-and-a-half. But despite the same tribal origins of their rulers, the two Emirates are very different.

Until the discovery of oil, the people of Abu Dhabi lived mainly in the desert and the oases.

Dubai Creek, heart of the city, is lined with multi-storey buildings.

The present modern city was scarcely more than a fishing village. The people of Dubai, however, had always been more settled around the excellent harbour provided by the creek. They had long concentrated on trade, and this talent was given a dynamic boost in the early part of the 20th century when many families emigrated to Dubai from Lingeh and neighbouring districts on the Persian coast. These families already had good trading links with their former homeland, and from that basis they built up a network of trade with India, Persia, East Africa, and the Gulf. They brought a more cosmopolitan atmosphere to the coastal towns of the Trucial States.

Abu Dhabi, and to a lesser extent Dubai, were to play the leading role in the massive expenditures involved in developing the country after independence, and in bringing it rapidly into the 20th century. Almost all the roads, schools, colleges, hospitals, ports and modern buildings in the land have been constructed since that time. The first two decades in the life of the United Arab Emirates must have seen more rapid and more extensive development than virtually any other country in the world (with the possible exception of Kuwait) can ever have known.

Since the burden of financing this development fell on Abu Dhabi, her capital was chosen as the provisional capital of the country as a whole, and her Ruler, HH Sheikh Zayed bin Sultan Al Nahyan, was elected President of the UAE. Dubai's previous Ruler, the late HH Sheikh Rashid bin Saeed Al Maktoum, was elected Vice President and Prime Minister of the new state. The Rulers of Sharjah, Ras Al Khaimah, Ajman, Fujairah and Umm Al Quwain became members of the controlling Supreme Council.

Some of these 'Northern Emirates', as they are collectively called, were also destined to experience the benefits of oil strikes in their territories, though never strikes on the scale of those of Abu Dhabi nor even of Dubai. Sharjah has so far been the most fortunate in the discovery of oil and gas, while Ras Al Khaimah has found some too. Prospecting continues in other areas of the UAE and with improved modern techniques may at any moment achieve further successes. Ultimately extensive development and modernisation in the UAE depends on the discovery of oil. Emirates which have found none have smaller populations and more rural towns than the oil-rich emirates with their extensive modern cities.

Flower borders in a Sharjah park.

Bank building in Abu Dhabi.

11

Fishing along the coasts was always an important source of livelihood.

Bedu of the Liwa Sands.

People of the UAE

Until the founding of the UAE, most of her people were of Arab tribal origin, members of tribes who had inhabited the land as far back, perhaps, as 2,000 years ago. They had controlled the deserts ever since, bred camels, cultivated the date palms in the small oases and mountain valleys, fished along the coastline, and each summer gone out to the pearling banks to collect pearls. Some had settled permanently in the small towns along the coast and engaged in maritime trade, with fluctuating fortunes over the centuries. All were sincere Muslims of the Sunni sect of Islam.

They were joined, as mentioned above, in the early part of this century, by merchant families from the southern shores of Iran. These families were mostly Sunni Muslims also, probably initially of Arab origin since these southern shores had often been ruled by the Qawasim in the past, and most pure Iranians are of the Shia sect. A few Indian merchants came to settle on the coasts too, again mostly in Dubai. From the 1950s there were other immigrants, Arabs from the northern Arab states, especially Palestinians, Lebanese and Syrians, who moved south to enjoy the peace and tranquillity of the Trucial States and escape disturbances in their homelands.

Nevertheless, the population of the country remained small, restricted as it was then by scant water resources and lack of infrastructure. In 1960 there were an estimated 100,000 people living in the country; at the census of 1968 there were found to be 180,000.

The vast development which followed the founding of the UAE completely changed the character of the small, quiet, essentially Arab towns of the coast. Foreign workers from Pakistan, India, the Philippines, Europe and the United States arrived in ever increasing numbers until, at the 1985 census, the population had soared to 1.6 million, a figure which has undoubtedly increased since then. The original Arab population of the UAE has expanded very fast too, with many families having eight or ten children, but nevertheless they are now thought to represent only a minority of the population, of which the great majority consists of immigrants.

However, the UAE does not experience the friction between peoples of different nations and races which is becoming commonplace in the west. With the exception of a few of the very earliest

Cosmopolitan building styles, like the windtowers here, came to Dubai early in the century.

arrivals, immigrants are not granted UAE nationality nor the right to stay forever. They come to do a job, and when the job is finished they go back home, often with much regret.

For life in the UAE, which before the days of air-conditioning was rated among the toughest in the world, is now considered to be among the most congenial. Subsidised electricity provides a comfortable environment in home, shop and office all year round. Desalinated water ensures a copious water supply which even allows for the greening of the cities and the creation of colourful gardens, parks and garden suburbs. The dynamism of the UAE economy, boosted by vast oil revenues and relieved by the end of conflict in the Gulf, is likely to attract a continuing flow of immigrants to participate in this fortunate prosperity throughout the years to come.

Copious supplies of desalinated water are used for the creation of colourful gardens like these at Sharjah's airport.

The fountain on Khalid Lagoon is one of the highest in the world. It plays against a backdrop of the luxury Holiday International Hotel, the Marbella Club and the elegant modern Corniche Plaza office buildings.

AROUND THE EMIRATE

Sharjah is the only Emirate in the UAE with territory on both the country's east and west coasts. It thus enjoys a refreshing range of very varied landscapes, with some of the country's most popular picnic and leisure areas. With 2,600 square kilometres of desert, mountain and coastal terrain, it is small wonder that Sharjah was the pioneer in developing tourism and adventure excursions in the early 1980s.

On the west coast, Sharjah's territory stretches from the borders of Dubai to those of Umm Al Quwain, lapping around the Emirate of Ajman on the way. Inland it runs across some magnificent desert scenery and major wadis (valleys) to reach the fertile alluvial plains at the foot of the mountains, and thence on to hidden mountain valleys sheltering fields of intensely vivid green.

Sharjah town

The town of Sharjah has mushroomed during the past two decades, extending from a close cluster of houses and narrow lanes along the creek front, to absorb the coastal villages of Al Khan, Fasht and Hira and to extend to an area covering some 70 square kilometres. Meanwhile the population of the town grew from around 5,000 in 1960 to 20,000 in 1968 and more than 200,000 by 1990, by which time there were some 300,000 people in the Emirate as a whole. Today the heart of the town is still quite close to the creek, and the large and refreshing Khalid Lagoon which was dredged out at its inner end. Industrial districts and suburbs extend for many kilometres into the desert to the north and east.

Sharjah was the first town on the coast to commission a major town plan, drawn up by Halcrows in 1963. This plan has allowed for

The King Faisal Mosque.

Statue representing the 'rolla' tree above;
young banyan tree below.

wide open spaces such as the broad Al Rolla Square near the town centre, and for green areas and parks like the Jazira Park on the island of Khalid Lagoon, as well as extensive gardens running round the shores of much of the lagoon. The green areas are particularly popular with families who gather there for a stroll in the cool of the early evening, or sit on the grass to enjoy a cup of coffee. Municipal gardening reaches ambitious heights, with a prominent set of flower beds near the souqs (traditional markets) spelling out the city's motto, 'Smile you are in Sharjah', in both Arabic and English.

The tall fountain blowing a mist of spray across the centre of Khalid Lagoon is 100 metres high, the third highest in the world, coming close after the famous fountain on Geneva Lake, and the recent one in Jeddah. Close by the Khalid Lagoon is one of Sharjah's most prestigious buildings, the Central Market, better known as the 'New Souq' until a newer souq, in the shape of the fine Souq Al Majarra, was built on the edge of the creek in the late 1980s. Near the new souq, one of the town's major sculptures, the seven-branched pearl monument on Ittihad Square, was unveiled on National Day of 1989, to symbolise the unity of the seven Emirates. Close by, the impressive King Faisal Mosque reflects Sharjah's friendship with another important neighbour, Saudi Arabia.

Al Rolla Square is more urban in design than the lagoon gardens, its alleys flanked by stone columns brought to Sharjah from India back in 1926. In the centre of the square is a modern sculpture representing a tree, a reminder of the the great old rolla tree (a banyan tree), said to have been 200 years old, which once stood on this site. The tree was a centre for local gatherings and festivals, with its spreading branches providing welcome shade. It was removed when the town centre was being redeveloped, but rows of little rolla trees have been planted around the square to take its place.

From the western end of Rolla Square the modern Al Burj Avenue runs westwards to the creek. This road is named after an old watch-tower which still stands proudly on a roundabout in the middle of the road. The tower is all that remains of the once-magnificent husn, the Ruler's fort-cum-palace, which stood on this site until the late 1960s. The tower is quite overshadowed by the rows of identical high-rise office blocks on either side of the road. This is the street of

Aerial photo showing extensive development of Sharjah in the early 1990s. (Photo: Maps Geosystems, P.O. Box 5232 Sharjah)

In the cloth souq.

Sharjah Creek.

Al Khan Creek.

banks, and almost every block houses the prestigious offices of a bank on its ground floor, with other offices, often of government departments, on the upper floors.

Near the creek, Al Burj Avenue cuts across the line of the old souq, running parallel to the banks of the creek. Small sections of this souq survive today, retaining their characteristic aromas of spices, incense, rose water and coffee. Now the old souq is separated from the bustle along the creek side by a wide corniche road which follows the coast northwards all the way to the borders of Ajman. In the creek itself a line of dhows (local wooden boats) jostle for space, their cargoes piled along the wharves awaiting loading. Across the water, on the far bank of the creek, the modern installations of the port and power station rise above the low Layyah sandspit.

Inland a little, and parallel to the creek, runs one of the town's main arteries, Al Arooba Street, a permanently busy business centre. This was the town's first modern artery, created in the late 1960s when it formed part of the main road running north from Dubai to Ras Al Khaimah, the country's first hard-top highway. Here the first high-rise modern buildings were constructed, and the first roundabout was inaugurated. It is still a major business street, featuring offices, banks and tourist companies. Towards its southern end this street runs up onto a very long flyover, crossing over the end of the creek and the edge of Khalid Lagoon, to come downwards again towards yet another creek, the once extensive Al Khan Creek on Sharjah's southern border with Dubai.

Here, amazingly, on a spit of sand between the creek and the sea, the old village of Al Khan has remained almost intact with its watchtowers and old coral houses, only a stone's throw it seems from the large modern buildings of Dubai on the one side, and Sharjah on the other. The shifting sandbanks at the entrance of this creek are a clear demonstration of the hazards to which creeks along this coast were always subject, for Al Khan Creek was once a major maritime refuge. On its shores the traditional wooden dhows, which have plied these waters since time immemorial, are still built in a small, attractively sited dhow yard. Some three or four craft are usually under construction there at any one time. The dhow builders work with the traditional tools of the past (hammer, saw and adze being the main ones) and attach the planking to the keel before fitting the ribs inside the planked hull.

Fishing dhow under construction on the banks of Al Khan Creek. These dhows are built by age-old techniques from teak wood imported from India.

Inland of the creek stand the striking red and white striped domes of the Expo centre. Now a major cultural and recreational development is planned for the banks of Al Khan Creek which will be dredged and the tidal flats around it filled in. A second branch to the creek is also planned, opening between Dubai's Al Mamzar Creek and the main Al Khan waterway.

The whole area will be laid out with pleasant gardens and cultural buildings, to complement Dubai's seaside park on the sand bar between Al Mamzar inlet and the sea, and to form a suitable setting for the village of Al Khan which has been designated a conservation area. A canal is also planned to link Al Khan Creek and Khalid Lagoon, to improve the circulation of water through both.

On the fine sandy beach to the north of Al Khan stand several of Sharjah's leading tourist hotels. The setting is superb on this quiet stretch of coast, yet so close to two of the country's major cities. The Carlton Hotel, nearest to Al Khan, was one of

The new Al Qassemi Hospital.

The Grand Hotel stands on a fine beach.

Swiss chalet in Sharjah.

the country's first luxury hotels, when it was built in the early 1970s. At that time it stood all alone on a magnificent, untouched sandy beach, with just a scatter of palm trees and palm-frond huts among the sand dunes. Today's urban development has engulfed this sandy stretch too, reaching almost to the doors of the Carlton and the neighbouring Grand Hotel.

The main road from Dubai runs inland of Al Khan Creek, engineered across land that was frequently waterlogged in the past (until the road was built in the 1960s) and even today at periods of very high tides or heavy rain. The modern, dual carriage highway stands clear of any flooding. The highway runs directly due north, into Al Wahda Street, a major thoroughfare which divides Sharjah's extensive industrial areas on the east of the town from the town centre to the west. Al Wahda Street is now the principal shopping street of the town, with fashion boutiques, Italian shoe shops, crystal and gift shops, and numerous cafés and restaurants along its southern section; while the northern sector specialises in furniture and furnishings. Follow this road northwards and it comes eventually to the Culture Roundabout in the northern suburbs, the site of several of Sharjah's newest and most prestigious buildings. Here is the elegant, green-fronted cultural centre, the fine heritage centre, and the new City Hall and Ruler's Office building. Near the park, behind the Cultural Centre, stands Sharjah's answer to Swiss Cottage — a new chalet-villa of the northern suburbs. Nearby too is the fine modern Al Qassemi Hospital.

From this roundabout the main artery turns off to the east, the highway to Sharjah's elegant airport, some 10 kilometres inland and close to the vital Al Saja'a Oilfield. Development of the town is now reaching out towards the airport, and indeed is scheduled to absorb all the land to the south of the airport road. Beyond the airport the road runs on inland, past the new National Park, and then on across the ochre sands to the green oasis of Dhaid.

The desert

The stretch of desert between Sharjah town and Jebel Faya, the rocky forerunner of the great Hajar Mountains, is one of the most popular areas of sand dunes in the country. The sand here is fine, fading from a pale cream colour near the coast to deep orangey red near the mountains. The dunes are short and steep, a challenge to adventurous desert drivers. Outcrops of the Jebel Faya provide welcome shade at midday, a stimulating place in which to scramble with the chance of finding ancient fossil shellfish embedded in the rock.

Here at the foot of the dunes the people of a little Bedouin village keep camels and goats and there is a constant scene of traditional activity as their animals scramble up the steep sand cliffs above the houses. Their village near the foot of the Jebel (mountain) is the successor to far more ancient settlements. Rock-built tombs, thousands of years old, dot the flanks of the mountain, and under its shade on the eastern side lay an extensive town in the days of the Greeks and Romans. This was the line between the desert and the sown, the point where sand dunes stop abruptly in a clear-cut golden cliff.

Closer in to Sharjah town lies another favourite desert area, a low valley among the sands where a copse of willowy ghaf trees grows happily among the dunes, and where water stands in shallow pools after the winter rains. Here on Fridays family groups cluster under the trees for a picnic, while the children hurtle up and down on their hair-raising power-driven dune buggies.

Desert hyacinths flowering in the sands in winter.

The fine dunes lapping up to rocky Jebel Faya have a deeper colour closer to the mountains.

Winter rains create lakes among the ghaf trees.

The plain

The plain along the foot of the mountains has built up gradually over thousands of years from the rock and gravel washed down by the rains from the mountain slopes behind. For some 350 days a year the whole area is bone dry, the wadis cutting across the plain no more than irritating indents, which nearer the mountains present serious obstacles to passing vehicles. But on the remaining few days of the year the scene can change dramatically, and even frighteningly. Rain accumulates on the mountains, trickles become floods, cascades and roaring torrents. Animals, vehicles, and even badly sited houses can be swept away.

Such floods as one occasionally sees today

Before the construction of flood-control systems, the wadi at Madam was hazardous to traffic after heavy rains.

Camels are still used for transport in the desert.

Flocks of sheep browse in the sands.

(and probably far worse in wetter periods of the distant past) were responsible for creating the plains. Scientists have calculated that the first layers were deposited during the Pleistocene period (the 'Ice Age' which began half-a-million years ago); another very wet period followed around 30,000 years ago when a further layer was built up, then again another some 8,000 years ago. The process is continuing today, though much more slowly in the present dry climate.

Beneath the plain lie reservoirs of sweet water, accumulated from the mountains perhaps thousands of years ago. Wells sunk down to this water suffice to nourish extensive fields of fruit and vegetables. In the ancient city near Mleiha a well more than 2,000 years old was found. It

The old fort at Dhaid once guarded the precious falaj.

went down to about the same depth as the wells of thirty years ago, before the widespread use of pumps lowered the water table in the plain.

The great oasis of Dhaid, with its rich palm groves and mile upon mile of cultivated farms, has been one of the first to suffer from the falling water table. Once the palm groves were fed by an underground water conduit, a falaj, which was said to be one of the most prolific falajes in the land. This falaj was protected by an old mud-brick fort in whose courtyard were some of the shafts leading down to the water. Soon after passing under the fort, the falaj emerged above ground among the palm trees, and separated shortly into five little streams leading off among the palm trees. Each farmer had a daily time share of the water's flow, and had to close off his stream when his time was up. Today the falaj still emerges near the remains of the old fort behind its successor, the modern police station, but the flow is reduced to a mere trickle which is supplemented by water from the mains.

On the Mleiha Road out of Dhaid is a new camel race track, where races are held throughout the winter months. Camel camps can often be seen on the dunes to the west of the oasis,

Camels exercising on the new race track in the sands.

24

The dramatic folds of the arid Hajar Mountains hide emerald green valleys where a trickle of water can be found.

while after the races strings of camels trek off home along the roads which converge on the oasis.

The mountains

The Hajar range forms a spine of arid, rocky mountains running the length of the east coast of the UAE and right down through Oman to far south of Muscat as well. These mountains are thought to have been pushed up over the land in ancient times, from under the seabed to the east. They consist of a jumbled mass of rocks of different origin, some sedimentary, some volcanic, mixed together in places like the layers of a cake. Geologists think the mountains have been there for some 70 million years, and that they are still rising very slowly.

Minerals are sometimes found there in the rocks of volcanic origin, and this is the case in one of Sharjah's southern wadis, Wadi Helou.

There in the centre of the wadi, a watchtower stands by the traces of an abandoned village in whose walls are to be found occasional pieces of the jet-black stones of copper slag. A path up the hillside above is littered with small pieces of green-tinged stone, the ore from an ancient copper mine. Many of these ancient mines are to be found throughout the Hajar Mountains, but very few of them are thought to contain copper in commercial quantities today. In most cases the ancient miners did their job too thoroughly in the past.

Today in most of the wadis, the people have moved down to new villages near the mouth of the wadi, where access is easier by vehicle, and from which their children can go to school. Even those who have remained in the heart of the mountains, as in the remote villages of Nahwa and Shees near the east coast, today have the benefit of electricity, a motor track, and visiting medical services.

Khor Fakkan, built around its beautiful bay, enjoys one of the finest natural settings of any town in the Emirates.

THE EAST COAST

The east coast of the Emirates is scenically the most beautiful part of the whole country. High steep mountains drop in rocky folds directly into the clear blue waters of the Gulf of Oman. Broad bays enclose sheltered palm groves with villages huddling close to their trees. Fine stretches of golden beaches line these bays, beaches which are often a scene of intense activity by the local fishermen, as well as a favourite picnicking spot for weekends and holidays. This coastline also provides the best snorkelling and underwater diving with brilliantly coloured fish weaving their way among intricate coral formations.

Until very recent times the east coast was almost separated from the rest of the country by the great barrier of the Hajar Mountains. A tortuous route existed through the broad and rocky Wadi Ham, running down from Masafi to Fujairah, and another, even more tortuous track could be picked out along Wadi Tayyibah northwards to Dibba. Along the coast itself each town and village was separated from the next by a spur of rock which ran down to the sea, and must be painfully traversed before the next bay could be reached.

Today excellent roads have been engineered over the mountains, the one following Wadi Ham, the other parallel to Wadi Tayyibah, and the two linked by a scenic coast road giving spectacular views along its whole length. A round trip to the east coast is a favourite outing for inhabitants of the cities of the west coast.

Despite its remoteness, the east coast always enjoyed a strategic importance in the past. Its towns offered sheltered harbours to ships coming in from the Indian Ocean, and access was good through the deep waters at the foot of the mountains. This coastline was far more approachable than the low sandy shore,

27

The Bay of Dibba was compared for its beauty with the Bay of Naples.

mingling imperceptibly with shallow waters and sandbanks, along the west coast.

Good harbours were always at a premium on this major crossroads of some of the world's busiest maritime trade routes. When the Portuguese galleons sailed into these waters early in the 16th century, the harbours of the east coast were among their first targets. Alfonso de Albuquerque stormed the port of Khor Fakkan; he described the place as a large town with a good harbour, temperate and healthy climate, plenty of sweet water and extensive cultivation. The people of the time grew wheat, millet, oranges, limes, dates, figs and plantains. They exported large numbers of horses across the sea to India, and Khor Fakkan was said to be the first place where oranges were cultivated, west of the Indian Ocean.

For many centuries this coastline was disputed, until eventually an agreement was concluded that it should belong to the Qawasim. In the past few years the importance of these harbours on the east coast has again been brought into prominence, when many ships chose to unload there rather than steam into the troubled waters of the Gulf.

Dibba

Sharjah's most northerly port on the east coast is the beautiful and historic little town of Dibba. In fact this town is divided into three sections of which Sharjah owns the central one, Husn Dibba. The old Portuguese plans also show the town already divided into three sections, much as it is today. Husn Dibba has been developed with a corniche road and good fishing harbour with space for 160 boats. It is the centre of intense activity, with fishing boats heading out into Dibba's beautiful open bay, surrounded by a backdrop of sheer umber-coloured mountains. It was described by a traveller in the last century as a bay as fine as that of Naples. Along the beach on either side of the harbour teams of fishermen may often be seen hauling in their long seine nets to take the catch of anchovies or sardines, whose shoals come close into shore in winter.

Dibba's fine natural position has attracted settlers since ancient times. Daggers, arrowheads, pottery and bone buttons made some 3,000 years ago were found by chance just inland of the town

28

in the 1960s. The green palm groves, which fringe the town, must already have existed in those times.

By the time that the revelation of Islam came to the area, Dibba was the capital of all Oman. But it was also the seat of a rebellion by the Azd tribe and their allies against Islam, after the death of the Prophet Muhammed (Peace be upon him). Three armies were sent from Mecca by the Caliph Abu Bakr in 632 AD, to suppress this revolt. Two of them reached Dibba and a great battle was engaged outside the town. The battle raged evenly all day, but in the late afternoon the third Muslim army arrived having come via Bahrain. The tide of battle swung in their favour, and many of the rebels were killed. Dibba was sacked, never to regain its former pre-eminence. On the plain behind the town, in a barren area of desert thorn trees, a vast cemetery of silent standing stones still marks the spot where some 10,000 dead from the battle are said to lie buried.

Fishing is still the livelihood of many of Dibba's people.

Along the beach, in front of the town, teams of fishermen pull in seine nets, trapping shoals of sardines or anchovies.

29

The beautiful wadi leading to the remote village of Shees.

The beach of the Oceanic Hotel is a favourite resort.

Khor Fakkan

South of Dibba, Sharjah's next town on the east coast is set on the picturesque bay of Khor Fakkan (Creek of the two Jaws). This bay, as its name implies, is far more enclosed than that of Dibba, and the town is more compact. The old town is concentrated at the southern end of the bay (although the old Portuguese fort was recorded at the northern end). Modern development, however, has extended the attractive town all round the bay which is lined with gardens, small cafés and a corniche road. A fine, white souq with ornate plaster work decoration and tall windtowers, stands at the centre of the bay, while a palace crowns a rocky eminence near the beach to the north of it. At the foot of the enclosing mountains to the north of the bay, a large modern hotel, the Oceanic, stands right on the beach, a focal point for weekend and holiday visitors.

In the deep water of the southern section of Khor Fakkan Bay a modern port has been erected, its tall cranes rising as it seems from the water. This port has become increasingly busy in recent years, as a result initially of the Gulf wars; by the time peace was established shipping lines had realised the advantages of unloading on the east coast, saving several days of journey time.

Inland of Khor Fakkan the barren mountains rise steeply, their folds enclosing a number of fertile valleys where little villages have eked a living from traditional agriculture along terraces fashioned in the wadi sides. They grow date palms, vegetables and sweet corn, limes and mangoes, and fodder for animals. High up in one of these wadis the modern Rifaisa Dam has been constructed to check the flood waters and provide a reservoir for use by the town.

In another Sharjah wadi, which leads to the little mountain village of Shees, sweet water is also available year round in a series of beautiful rock pools. The villagers have constructed rocky conduits from this natural source, to bring water to their village on a ridge above the pools, and to their fields on narrow terraces below. But they still suffer from occasional fierce floods which can wash out the motor track to the village, leaving the wadi strewn with giant boulders. A continuous effort is needed to keep the route open and when it is not, helicopters bring relief to the village.

Khor Fakkan's new souq is one of the
most elegant in the Emirate.

Fishing by line is a popular pastime for boys of the East Coast.

Kalba

To the south of Fujairah lies another stretch of Sharjah territory with the villages of Kalba and Khor Kalba. Here the plain is wider between the mountains and the sea and there is more scope for agriculture. These, too, are long standing settlements although Kalba was more often known as 'Ghallah' in the past. Today this large village has been considerably developed with dual carriage highways, roundabouts and modern shops and houses. It is still a centre of considerable fishing activity, with boats and nets pulled up on the beach.

Khor Kalba, the most southerly village before the border with Oman, is well sited by the northern shore of a particularly fine creek. Close to the creek is a recently opened motel with little red roofed chalets looking out over the water. A wide road bridge across the creek gives access to fine picnicking areas along the southern shore. For this creek shelters one of the best and most accessible mangrove swamps in the UAE. In the past many of the creeks had mangroves growing

Sharks' fins for export are hung up to dry in the sun at Khor Kalba.

Khor Kalba has one of the few remaining mangrove swamps in the country. (Inset: mangrove fruit and leaves)

Goats find sustenance even in the most rugged terrain.

in the shallow water along their shores. Today most of these thickets have disappeared, but that of Khor Kalba flourishes still. The mangroves were first described by a Greek geographer more than 2,000 years ago. He is quoted thus: "along the whole coast (of the Gulf) in the deep part of the water, grow trees resembling the laurel and the olive. When the tide ebbs the whole trees are visible above the water, and at full tide they are sometimes entirely covered. This is the more singular because the coast inland has no trees."

The mangroves provided poles which were widely used for roofing timbers, and for the masts of ships until quite recent times. In old houses one can still see the smooth round beams of mangroves, known as 'chandel poles', frequently bound round with cords to give purchase in the coral and gypsum walls. But mangroves, which grow to five metres or so high, are sensitive to their environment; if the ebb and flow of the tide is cut off, or the water much polluted, the whole thicket may die. The extensive mangrove swamp of Khor Kalba is indeed a fortunate survival.

THE PEOPLE AND THEIR CULTURE

The National Park of Sharjah is alive with people on Fridays and public holidays throughout the year. Families spread a cloth on the grass and picnic in the shade of the trees, children rush about in pursuit of colourful kites or footballs, smoke curls gently skywards from dozens of little barbecues. Although this park, a dozen kilometres out of town on the road towards Dhaid, only opened to the public in 1989, it has already become a favourite place in which to relax at the end of the week, a great treat for children of all ages. Here there are swings and playhouses, a little farm for local animals like goats and donkeys, and best of all a giant slide which curves its way down a large specially constructed sand dune.

The park is the best place in which to meet the people of Sharjah. Enjoying themselves in this beautiful setting, they reveal many of the characteristics of their community as a whole. They are sociable and hospitable; the family groups do not seek the seclusion of a distant lawn, but cluster together on the main lawns near the entrance. Their children play in happy flocks; friends come across to partake of a cup of coffee (a thermos flask is the first essential of every picnic) or stay for the barbecue.

Born in a desert environment, they are especially fond of flowers and greenery. In this they share the tastes of their Ruler, HH Dr Sheikh Sultan bin Mohammed Al Qasimi, who himself has a degree in agriculture and whose love of gardening has been the inspiration for many delightful parks in Sharjah.

At sunset people can be seen praying among the trees, or by the roadside on the way back into Sharjah. This has always been a strongly Islamic Emirate; adherence to the tenets of their religion is

Men performing a traditional dance in Ittihad Square in front of the New Souk. (Photo: Dariush Zandi)

35

A decorative minaret near Sharjah Creek.

of great importance to the community. They take a lead in caring for those members of their society who are less able to look after themselves. Hence an attractive old people's home has been opened on the beach at Layyah, in a fine natural setting yet within easy reach of the town. The sick are treated at the large, modern Al Qassemi Hospital, in the north of the city; Sharjah also has one of the country's best private hospitals, the Al Zahra. The Kuwaiti Hospital, which dates from the early days of public health care, is now a maternity hospital. There is an impressive school for deaf and handicapped children, the Sharjah City for Humanitarian Services, professionally run by a senior member of the ruling family.

Education

The earliest school, based on traditional Islamic methods, was opened in Sharjah in 1903, by a wealthy local pearl merchant, Ali Al Mahmud. This school, the Taimiyyah, was a large school taking 200 boys from Sharjah and 120 as boarders

Schoolboys on their way home from school — a daily scene for all the Emirate's children.

from the Northern Emirates. Schooling and accommodation were provided free of charge. Ali Al Mahmud invited eminent maths teachers from other Arab countries to come to teach at his school in Sharjah, and in 1911 he opened another school in Hamriyah.

In 1953 the first school to teach on modern lines in the whole country was opened in Sharjah; it gave Sharjah a flying start in education, and also provided schooling for many of the merchants' sons from Dubai. Older men from that city recall the difficult trek around the waterlogged lagoons (a journey which now takes five minutes by car), and the delightful unexpected days off school when the tide rose too high for them to cross the tidal flats.

The first girls' school was opened in Sharjah, too, and by the late 1960s Sharjah still had the only girls' secondary school in the land. Technical education started here as well, with the country's first trade school being started in Sharjah back in 1958. As a result of this early start in schooling, Sharjah has an educated, middle-aged generation who have played a leading role in such UAE Ministries as those of Education and Foreign Affairs.

Now that all her children have schooling readily accessible, Sharjah has been able to turn her attention to the education of children with special needs. A school for deaf children was opened in 1980 and has since been greatly expanded over the years. Today the City for Humanitarian Services, under its dedicated director Sheikha Jamila Al Qasimi, caters for some 350 children altogether, about half of whom are deaf, and the others with mental or physical handicaps. A branch has been opened in Khor Fakkan for children from the east coast, and there is a boarding section in Sharjah for deaf children from distant towns and villages.

Deaf children are taught here by the most modern methods of complete communication, using headphones and hearing aids, mime, lip-reading, sign language, music and vibration. Their classes are extremely moving on account of the intense concentration on the eager faces of the young students. At the end of the day they may join some of the lucky graduates of the school who have found regular jobs with banks, newspapers or been offered office work at the military base. But competition from the great numbers of graduates of the country's many secondary schools, colleges and university makes job-hunting particularly tough for them.

Friday on the East Coast and a schoolboy takes to fishing.

A deaf boy learning to speak with powerful modern hearing aids, at the City for Humanitarian Services.

37

Insignia of Sharjah's TV, the newest in the country.

A traditional tobacco-seller smokes a narghileh in front of his little shop in the beautifully reconstructed old souq, near the Sharjah Creek.

Department of Culture and Information

Sharjah's Culture Department also focuses on the needs of the Emirate's children, organising an annual children's cultural festival, providing children's libraries and producing children's books. This focus is taken up also by Sharjah's new television station, which produces daily programmes both for, by and about children.

Sharjah Television, the most recently opened in the UAE, began broadcasting in February 1989, and straight away won the 1990 award for the best locally produced programme in the UAE. The station produces a high proportion of its own programmes, seeking especially to broadcast programmes of value, both educationally and culturally. The station broadcasts eight hours a day in its Arabic service and two hours a day in Urdu. Where imported, English-language programmes are screened, they are often documentaries, dubbed or sub-titled in Arabic.

Children and education are also a major concern at the international Book Fair organised each year by the Department of Culture and Information and held in Sharjah's Expo Centre whose large domed halls are completely filled by rows and rows of book stalls. This is the region's major book fair and visitors from all over the Gulf region come to buy. It is particularly popular with local people who throng the halls until late in the evening, accounting for the exhibition's seven to ten thousand visitors a day. Leading exhibitors at the fair are Egypt, Syria and Lebanon and most of the books displayed are in Arabic, although there are many English-language scientific books, as well as a general section of English and some French books. Many families bring their children who are attracted by the colourful children's books on display, and by the chance to try their hand at a little artwork of their own.

Children again are some of the most eager participants at the numerous shows and events organised by the Department of Culture and Information at the fine new Cultural Centre on the Culture Roundabout at the start of the airport road. This beautiful building houses an excellent theatre with comfortable seating in the auditorium. Sharjah's four amateur dramatic groups play there, and troupes of actors are also brought in from abroad. Sharjah gave a major boost to local amateur drama by holding the Emirates' first, four-month theatre workshop in the town, back in 1982.

Schools make sure that their pupils get the chance to experience the broad range of cultural activities offered by the Centre. Take a London group's performance of a Shakespeare play, for example. The large hall is packed to overflowing and half to two-thirds of the audience are children or young people. Although the performance is in English they follow it intently, just longing to take part and joining in with effervescent enthusiasm the moment there is any clapping, singing

The International Book Fair at the Sharjah Expo Centre is one of the most popular events of the year.

The elegant new Cultural Centre attracts many of the city's young people.

'Lantern' by Husain Sharif.

In the courtyard of the Naboodah house.

or dancing on the stage. So magnetic is the attraction of the bright lights for some of the smaller members of the audience that they creep closer and closer to the stage, and by the final curtain call a row of little boys may actually be seen sitting spellbound along its edge.

Sharjah is also the headquarters of an active Fine Arts Association which brings together many of the country's leading painters and sculptors. These artists hold an annual arts exhibition and the Department of Culture organises an international 'arts biennale', bringing painters from some 30 foreign countries, to further encourage the fine arts in Sharjah. The Fine Arts Association also enables its members to participate in exhibitions in other Arab countries and indeed even further afield.

The Culture Department has also organised a recurrent National Arts Festival at the Expo Centre, focusing on folklore, crafts and ethnography. Collections of local songs and folklore are being amassed and the Festival is being transferred to the appropriate setting of some of the city's fine old houses which have been renovated in the early 1990s.

This renovation of Sharjah's architectural heritage is one of the most visible and significant of the Department of Culture's undertakings. With the introduction of modern building materials such as cement and plate glass in the 1960s, and the advent of considerable wealth in the 1970s, all the towns along the Emirates' coastline swept away their old districts which were most conveniently located on the creek side or shoreline, and replaced them with modern, concrete highrise buildings. By the late 1980s very little was left anywhere along the coast of the attractive old traditional architecture which had once given these towns their distinctive character.

Fortunately in Sharjah a little of the old souq remained intact behind the modern buildings on the creek front, and a few of the fine old merchants' houses were not completely dilapidated so as to allow for renovation. Most surprisingly of all, Sharjah still had an almost intact old fishermen's village on the promontory of Al Khan, a village complete with two or three watchtowers, coral-built houses, and its own unspoilt creek, a perfect example of the style of creeks and settlements before the oil era. This village too is now scheduled for conservation.

In the town itself, the first house to be restored was the fine, two-storey house of the Naboodah family. The courtyard of this house is surrounded by elegant wooden fluted columns, brought over — one old neighbour recalls — from India by the cloth merchant Obaid Al Naboodah. Close by this house a complete enclosed souq, grouping a number of little shops around a winding lane which could be closed off by heavy wooden doors at night, was also renovated in the early 1990s.

Archaeological techniques of excavation have revealed the foundations of further parts of the souq and neighbouring houses, and have brought to light a commercial date store, whose large ridged floor was used to hold dates for the production of date honey. Work in this area will also encompass one of the country's most original surviving windtowers, the well-known circular windtower on the old Midfa family house behind the traditional silver souq.

An even more ambitious project may be the reconstruction of the old husn or fort of Sharjah, which once stood on the site of Al Burj Avenue. The single tower on the roundabout of this busy thoroughfare is all that remains of the once-impressive fort, demolished in the late 1960s. Its reconstruction would restore to Sharjah one of its most impressive ancient monuments.

Unusual round windtower on the old Midfa family house.

The Midfa house before renovation.

Oil rig in the Mubarak Field. (Courtesy Crescent Petroleum)

OIL AND GAS

The first oil concession for Sharjah territory was signed by the Ruler back in 1938, on similar lines to concessions for the other emirates. They were, however, soon overtaken by the upheavals of the Second World War which delayed any chance of prospecting in the region for a couple of decades. In fact prospecting in Sharjah territory only commenced in 1962 (about the time that oil was first produced in Abu Dhabi territory), and then it was for an offshore concession, in the neighbourhood of the Sharjah-owned island of Abu Musa in the Gulf. Abu Musa was an inhabited island, some 80 kilometres offshore, and had been the centre of a thriving production of red oxide, a colouring used in making paint and cosmetics. At its height, the industry had produced some 16,000 tons of red oxide a year, but had declined seriously by the time oil was sought in the region. The seas near Abu Musa are also known for the production of cigales, the local flat-headed crayfish which are a favourite winter delicacy in the region.

Mubarak Field

The original concessionaries failed to find oil and in 1967 the concession was taken up by Buttes Gas and Oil. Soon Crescent Petroleum was founded as operator for Buttes and others in a consortium. In late 1972 oil was struck in the Mubarak Field, 12 kilometres off Abu Musa, and in the following year several more strikes were made in the same field. By 1974 production started at Mubarak, initially at a rate of about 20,000 barrels a day. Mubarak oil has a low sulphur content and is therefore popular on world markets.

The initial rate of production built up rapidly and was held at around 35,000 barrels a day for

Work in progress on Mubarak rig. (Courtesy Crescent Petroleum)

the first few years of the field's life. Subsequently, the flow declined in the early 1980s, to some 10,000 bpd and then to around 5,000 bpd, and remained at that rate. Drilling started in 1990 into a structure containing gas and condensate which had been discovered a few years earlier. Both gas and crude oil production has increased since then. Drilling new wells in this structure, at a depth of 14,000 feet, is continuing.

Oil from the Mubarak Field brought sufficient wealth to Sharjah to finance the rapid expansion of the city in the 1970s, and the development of the Emirate as a whole. However, just before independence, negotiations were undertaken in the Gulf to settle Iranian claims to ownership of a number of islands, initially including Bahrain. In late 1971, during the last two days of British presence in the Gulf, the Iranians seized the small islands of the Tunbs from Ras Al Khaimah; a sharing agreement was worked out for Abu Musa which belonged to Sharjah. An agreement included sharing the Mubarak Field, ceding 50 per cent of oil revenues to Iran. Umm Al Quwain also received a

Liquid Petroleum Gas storage tanks.

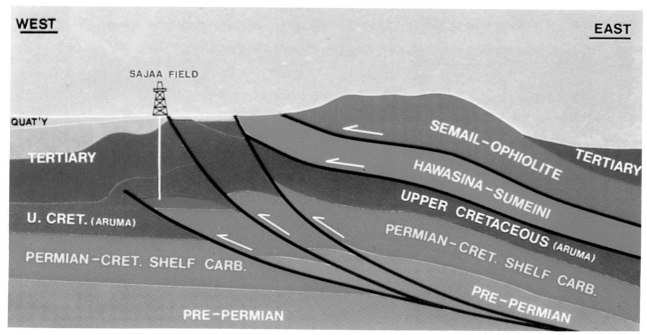

WEST

EAST

SAJAA FIELD

QUAT'Y

TERTIARY

SEMAIL-OPHIOLITE

TERTIARY

HAWASINA-SUMEINI

UPPER CRETACEOUS (ARUMA)

U. CRET. (ARUMA)

PERMIAN-CRET. SHELF CARB.

PERMIAN-CRET. SHELF CARB.

PRE-PERMIAN

PRE-PERMIAN

Plan of the fractured rock structures which gave rise to the Saja'a Field. (Courtesy Amoco)

small proportion of the revenues from Mubarak.

Efforts were also made to find oil offshore of Sharjah's east coast territories. A concession was granted in 1974 to Preserve Oil and Gas but their initial explorations were to no avail and they soon relinquished the concession. Other oil companies which took up the concession subsequently were to prove no more successful.

In 1978 a concession to prospect offshore between Hamriyah and Abu Musa was granted to Foreman Exploration and London and Scottish, and they struck gas in their concessionary area but later relinquished the concession.

Saja'a Field

Fortunately for Sharjah, hydrocarbons have also been discovered in its onshore territories. In 1979 an onshore concession was granted to Amoco, who explored the dunefield area between the west coast and the foot of the mountains. Here, in 1980, they struck gas at Saja'a, close to the Sharjah cement factory and just a little inland of the airport. At first sight, it may seem strange that the kind of domed rock structure — known as an anticline — in which oil is often found, should exist here in the middle of the flat, sand-covered plain. However, the powerful thrusting movements of the earth's crust which had pushed up the Hajar Mountains some 80 million years ago, had also shifted the rock sheets deep underground and far to the west of the mountains

Liquid Petroleum Gas recovery plant.

Saja'a plant process area.

themselves. Saja'a lies just above the western tip of one such thrust fault.

This rock dome was found to contain gas and high-quality condensate, a fine light crude oil which, once separated from the gas, sold well on world markets. A pipeline was built to Hamriyah, thence out to sea to deep water some 13 kilometres offshore. The first shipment of condensate was loaded there in 1982. At its peak, production of condensate built up to 60,000 barrels per day.

Meanwhile substantial facilities were required at Saja'a to handle separation of the gases and condensate. Shalco (the Sharjah LPG Company) was founded in 1984 to build a plant for the recovery of liquid petroleum gas — propane and butane. Shalco is owned 60 per cent by the Government of Sharjah, 25 per cent by Amoco, and 7.5 per cent each by two Japanese companies, C. Itoh Company and Tokyo Boeki. All the LPG produced is exported from Hamriyah. It is used as bottled gas for cooking, and is also especially useful as feedstock for petrochemical industries.

Some 10,000 barrels per day of LPG are currently produced at Saja'a. This gas is taken from the initial separation plant into Shalco's LPG plant, where it is cooled down to minus 78°C. At this temperature the propane, butane and remaining condensate can be separated; the liquid gases are then transferred to Hamriyah where they are stored in huge refrigerated tanks before being exported.

The other gases which are separated out at Saja'a are methane and ethane, known as dry gas. This gas is used to produce electricity and desalinated water for Sharjah and Dubai. A 75-kilometre-long pipeline has been built directly from Saja'a to Jebel Ali, to supply Dugas and the Dubai power station.

Currently some 350 million cubic feet a day of dry gas is produced at Saja'a. During the summer all this gas and more is needed to produce sufficient electricity to keep the country's air-conditioners functioning. In winter, however, when fewer people are using air-conditioning, the surplus gas is flared.

Production of condensate at Saja'a now stands at around 20,000 barrels per day, but for Sharjah as for its neighbour Dubai, the discovery of new fields would ensure its future prosperity. So far Sharjah has been fortunate: its birth as an independent state was welcomed by the discovery of oil at Mubarak; as production at Mubarak declined, the prosperous Saja'a field was discovered. Further discoveries could guarantee continued development and prosperity.

Saja'a's flare only burns brightly in winter, when demand for power is low and there is surplus gas.

Sharjah's Expo Centre hosts many exhibitions and trade fairs.

COMMERCE AND INDUSTRY

Sharjah has always been a trading town for as long as history relates. Her creek offered an excellent mooring for shallow draft wooden dhows, protected as it was behind the long sandspit of Layyah. Her people were always seafarers, fishermen, pearl divers and merchants. By the late 19th century Sharjah was rated the second most important port in the Gulf, following only after Kuwait. But the low-lying coast of the Emirates has always been subject to fickle currents, its creeks and inlets a real hostage to fortune.

Sharjah Creek

Sharjah's creek, on which the town's prosperity was based, began to suffer from severe silting in the mid-20th century, along with the neighbouring creeks of Dubai and Al Khan. Currents trending northwards along the coast began to pile more sand beyond the end of the protective spit, until sandbanks severely obstructed and finally virtually closed the mouth of the creek. For a while boats continued to enter, running in at high tide and waiting for another high tide to set out to sea again. But even that was difficult, for the sandbanks across the entrance to the creek shifted between one high tide and another.

Sharjah's creek was worse affected than that of Dubai; by the early 1950s dhows which used to call at Sharjah began to stop at Dubai instead. So Sharjah's leading position on the coast was gradually eroded. In the early 1970s a new entrance was cut through to the creek, near where the power station now stands. But this left the original creek as something of a backwater and the old creek mouth became more and more silted. So in 1975 the original entrance of the creek, near the Sharjah Continental Hotel,

Sharjah in 1976, showing silted creek mouth and the dredging of Khalid Lagoon. (Photo: Maps Geosystems, Sharjah)

was dredged; it was finally cleared of sand and has been kept clear ever since, while the temporary entrance was filled in again.

Today the extended creek has come alive once more and dhows jostle all along its quays. Although containers may carry the bulk of Sharjah's trade, it is these traditional dhows which

Drilling rigs under repair in Sharjah Creek.

are the most lively and colourful element in the life and commerce of the city. Merchants visit the ships, trucks bring their goods which are piled high along the wharves. There is a scene of constant activity on the creekside.

Ports and airport

Work started on the construction of the modern Port Khalid back in 1974. Previously a 700-metre-1ong jetty had been built out to sea from the Layyah sandspit back in 1965. Then a decade later moles were built out on either side of it along the sand bar, to enclose the area of the

Tugs waiting to go, under the shadow of a huge crane at Khor Fakkan's busy port. Activity at this East Coast port has increased dramatically in recent years.

present harbour. Deep water berths were constructed for large ships and the port became the first in the Middle East to take container cargoes, back in 1976. Although Port Khalid is faced with stiff competition since it lies so close to the larger harbours of Dubai and Jebel Ali, nevertheless, some two million tons of cargo pass across its quays each year.

Port Khalid is strongly supported by Sharjah's second modern port, over on the east coast at

A jewel of a mosque at Sharjah's airport.

The beautifully designed Sharjah International Airport provides an important air-sea freight link for Sharjah's foreign trade.

Khor Fakkan. Sharjah is the only Emirate to have ports on both east and west coasts, and has developed an efficient 'land bridge' linking the two. Goods landed at Khor Fakkan can be trucked across to Sharjah, remaining in bond if required. Thus Sharjah can take advantage both of shipping within the Gulf and of shipping remaining outside the Strait of Hormuz.

Khor Fakkan has the best natural deep water harbour in the whole region, and has therefore always been an important maritime port. The modern harbour, developed within the rocky bay, was opened back in 1979. For a decade its two berths could comfortably handle the cargo which came into the little town, but during the Iran-Iraq war the situation changed dramatically. Then shipping found that the risks and high insurance premiums for entering the Gulf made Khor Fakkan an attractive option. This feeling was reinforced during the second Gulf War following the invasion of Kuwait, and shipping lines began to call more and more frequently at Khor Fakkan. In 1991 Gulftainer, who manage both Sharjah's ports, reported record traffic and 260,000 containers unloaded at Khor Fakkan, where two powerful new cranes were added to supplement the existing two. Shipping lines reckon they can save two days' sailing time if they unload at Khor Fakkan, instead of sailing round into the Gulf and unloading at one of the ports on the west coast of the UAE.

The ports work in close cooperation with Sharjah International Airport, providing a strong air-sea freight link. Air cargo being moved through the airport is increasing very rapidly, and has reached some 8,000 tons a month. Sharjah airport is quite the most attractive one in the country, a neat compact design of a series of low domes, with elegant spires flanking the central dome on either side. It was opened in 1977, to take over from the old airport, the country's first one, which by that time had been engulfed by the growing town around it. Even the new airport is not far away from the centre of the town, being only some 18 kilometres from Port Khalid.

Sharjah's merchants carry on a flourishing trade with Iran, Kuwait and other Gulf states, as well as with the nations of Europe, the United States, and the Far East. The entrepot trade is of particular importance here, since Sharjah stands at a cross-road of world trade. More goods are exported in the way of transit trade than as direct exports from Sharjah itself.

Modern cranes load and unload an endless procession of colourful containers at Khor Fakkan Port.

Swimming pools stacked on edge at Riviera Pool in Sharjah's industrial area.

The clean lines of Hempel's Marine Paints factory in Layyah.

Sharjah Cement Works occupies a large complex out beyond the airport, adjacent to the Saja'a Oilfield. It is one of Sharjah's biggest industries.

Industry

The visitor to Sharjah can easily find himself bemused since all road signs seem to point to 'Industrial Sector' in one direction or another, and at some roundabouts the signs offer 'Industrial Sector' in every direction. In fact this is not as confusing as it looks. Sharjah has dedicated a large sector in the south-eastern part of the town — some 18 square kilometres to date — to the creation of an extensive industrial zone. Here, streets are lined with small car workshops, with furniture factories, plastics factories and factories for metal work of one kind or another. Outside one factory piles of blue lined plastic swimming pools stand incongruously stacked on their sides; nearby a fibreglass 'dhow' rests uneasily by the roadside, or piles of colourful paint tins stand stacked ready for transit.

This policy of encouraging modest manufacturing units to set up shop in Sharjah has brought surprising results. There are already some 300 industrial units there with more than 10 employees each, which actually represent some 40 per cent of all the manufacturing units in the whole of the UAE. They cover a wide range of products too. Chemical and petrochemical products are in the lead, with plastics, fibreglass and paints playing major roles. Plastic bags, boxes and buckets add their own brilliant colours to the scene, while high-speed power boats provide a dash of excitement.

Building materials, naturally, make up a major sector of the market in a town which is expanding as rapidly as Sharjah. Metal doors and window frames, electrical cables and appliances, marble slabs and tiles, bricks and concrete blocks, bathroom fittings and bags of cement are the bases of this industrial sector. Indeed the cement works outside the town, a little beyond the airport, is one of Sharjah's largest factories. Limestone from the rocky ridges near Mleiha, some 50 kilometres to the east, is trucked to the factory and baked in a rotating kiln to produce dark grey clinker. This is then ground down in great drums with heavy metal balls rattling around in them, to form the cement which is bagged into sacks produced by the cement plant's own bag factory. Gas from the Saja'a Field, just close by across the desert, is used to power the kiln.

Another major industry is of course the production of electricity which is distributed to the population at subsidised rates. In a climate as hot as that of the UAE, the provision of air-

The Layyah power station, on the sandspit between Sharjah Creek and the sea, provides electricity for Sharjah town.

conditioning throughout the summer months is an absolute prerequisite of an advanced industrial society, and indeed of any kind of modern life. Sharjah has two power stations, one of them in Nasiriyah and the other prominently sited on the edge of the creek at Layyah. There are also power stations in Khor Fakkan and Kalba for the east coast region. In recent years street lighting has been installed all along the roads from Sharjah to Dubai and Sharjah to Dhaid, as well of course as throughout the urban areas.

Sharjah plays a leading role in the production of furniture, pre-fabricated accommodation blocks, and wooden products of all kinds. The beds, couches, tables and cupboards manufactured in the industrial zone can be purchased directly in the shops of Al Wahda Street, or are sold outside the Emirate. Selling outside too, and indeed exporting 90 per cent of their product, are the numerous garment factories which have opened in the

late 1980s. Some of these factories spin and weave the cloth which is then made up into fashionable clothes for sale abroad.

Foodstuffs, gold jewellery, basic metal products and animal fodder are all areas in which Sharjah manufacturers are active. One of the most ecologically sound of Sharjah's manufacturing ventures, however, is the garbage reprocessing unit which turns household refuse into agricultural fertilisers.

Business in Sharjah

Sharjah offers a range of benefits to investors which are normally only found in duty-free zones. The most significant of these is 100 per cent-foreign ownership for commercial and industrial ventures. This means that foreign businessmen may set up their enterprises anywhere in the Emirate of Sharjah and take advantage of the government's competitive business package,

Al Burj Avenue, the street of banks, with (inset) the entrance to the National Bank of Sharjah.

which also includes 100 per cent repatriation of profits and capital. Government officials calculate that foreign businessmen will find it considerably cheaper to set up business in Sharjah, since the cost of housing is notably lower than in the other major centres of Dubai and Abu Dhabi, and there is no requirement of a local partner owning 51 per cent of the business.

Sharjah has an extensive banking sector to handle any business needs, with 11 local and 18 foreign banks operating in the city. Like other banks in the UAE, they experienced a period of strain in the mid-1980s, when the decline in oil prices brought a recession in the Gulf. Sharjah banks managed to survive the difficult period which led to suggestions that the UAE as a whole was perhaps over-banked. Further problems for banks in the early 1990s, partly due to the Iraqi invasion of Kuwait, have also been survived by Sharjah banks with support from the UAE Central Bank. Sharjah bankers are now hopeful that delayed payments for large quantities of gas sold to the Emirates General Petroleum Company (EGPC) will eventually reinvigorate the financial sector.

A further asset for Sharjah businesses is the active Sharjah Expo Centre, which first started operations in 1977. The original Expo Centre was located close to the King Faisal Mosque, not far from the New Souq. It was moved in 1990 to a more open location on the southern edge of the city, nearest to Dubai, to attract visitors equally from both cities. The characteristic red and white striped, teflon-bonded canvas domed halls were considerably enlarged to include three long parallel halls and a separate smaller one. Exhibitions and trade fairs are organised there throughout the winter and include some events unique to the UAE, such as the highly popular autumn book fair. A new road link gives an easy direct access to the Expo Centre from the main Sharjah-Dubai road which passes close by it.

The flags of many nations fly gaily around the Sharjah Expo Centre for an international fair.

Surveying for the final touches to the approaches to Sharjah's Expo Centre, on the south side of the city.

The elegant New Souq, on the banks of Khalid Lagoon, is a favourite destination for shoppers from Sharjah and Dubai.

A WEALTH OF SOUQS

The souq was always the *raison d'etre* of the towns of the emirates. They were, in fact, from the earliest times, little market towns, importing goods such as rice, spices, pottery and fabrics from abroad, to sell to people of the interior, and exporting dates, limes and Arab horses in exchange. So the souqs were always built as close as possible to the harbour, along the banks of the creek or directly on the seashore as at Abu Dhabi. With the rapid development of modern cities over the past two decades, these same areas were prime land for commercial properties, hotels, corniche roads and so forth, with the result that many of the traditional souqs were swept away in the first rush of development. Today those emirates which still have sections of their old souqs surviving have come to appreciate that they are in fact a source of considerable attraction, and popular as shopping areas with local inhabitants and tourists alike.

Sharjah is now in the forefront of the move to conserve and restore as much as possible of her ancient souqs which once lined the inland shores of her lengthy creek. And Sharjah has also taken the lead in applying the finest of modern architectural ideas to the design of modern souqs, indeed of raising the construction of new souqs to an art form.

Fish and vegetable souqs

A number of food and animal souqs have been established along the inner edge of the creek, where it begins to widen into the Khalid Lagoon. Foremost of these is, of course, the fish souq, traditionally the most important of all the souqs in days gone by when families along the coast ate fish for their mid-day meal almost every day.

59

Red snappers being unloaded at the fish souq.

The fish souq stands just beside the bridge crossing the creek from Al Arooba Street towards the Jazira Island and Al Khan. Its buildings are of plain concrete, but the scene along the quay within is lively and colourful. Fishing dhows moor along the wharf, decanting their loads of freshly caught fish onto the quay. There the piles of fish are quickly auctioned, some being loaded into pick-up trucks for sale elsewhere, others being spread out on the fishmongers slabs along the open front of the buildings. Hamour, king-fish, red snappers, prawns and crayfish are among the favourites on sale, while brightly coloured smaller fish make a delicious dish grilled whole or barbecued. Although fresh fish is no longer quite the important staple of the local diet that it once was, the souqs of the UAE still offer some of the best fresh fish in the world.

Immediately across the road from the fish souq are the nicely designed, long low white buildings of the fruit and vegetable souq. Inside the long central corridor of this modern building are some 120 small fruit and vegetable stalls, while others spill over onto the open land outside, and present a colourful sight sheltering under their brightly striped sun umbrellas.

All along the dual carriageway from the vegetable souq to the bend in the creek, an impromptu new horticultural souq has sprung up under palm branch sun shades. Here stall after stall sells bougainvillaea and hibiscus plants, frangipani, oleander, datura and jasmine, all grown in little tins or black plastic bags and ready to transplant in burgeoning villa gardens. Thirty years ago there was hardly a blade of green along this coast, but today garden suburbs are springing up with mushroom speed.

At the corner of the creek an extensive animal souq entices would-be owners of chickens, rabbits, ducks and pigeons as well as more serious purchases such as sheep, goats, camels and horses. Groups of camels and horses can often be seen at the entrance to the souq, standing forlornly by the creekside awaiting a new owner.

The old souqs

Follow the corniche road just a little further round towards the sea and one comes to a row of high modern buildings lining the corniche. Tucked in behind them, however, are the low shops and shaded lanes of the old souq which in this section sells traditional silver jewellery,

Fresh fruit and vegetables on sale at the vegetable market.

daggers and antiques. Old wooden benches in the shade outside some of the shops are gathering places for the older inhabitants who sit and sip glasses of sweet tea and while away the day in gentle conversation.

These old souqs once continued some way inland but this area was abandoned over the past few decades and left to gradually crumble. Now an ambitious project of restoration has been undertaken, and one attractive group of souq stalls around an enclosed lane has already been completely rehabilitated.

The main old souq lane, running parallel to the creek, is cut through by the broad Al Burj Avenue but continues on the further side of that modern highway. Here, its nature changes somewhat. The stalls are piled with bags of spices, rice, nuts and coffee beans, some colourful with clothing fabrics and garments, or filled with household utensils. The narrow lane is almost completely covered over, providing a welcome shade in the heat of the day, and the souq is always alive with shoppers. Opening off this section of the

A quiet lane in the old souq.

Old souqs and new line the creek front.

Sharjah is one of the most favourable markets in the world for gold.

The colourful New Souq is a popular venue for purchases of all kinds.

souq are the old buildings of the Sarah Hosmon Hospital, one of the earliest hospitals to be founded in Sharjah, and set in the house of the former British political agent. For some 40 years this simple maternity hospital welcomed the new-born of Sharjah, giving them a safer start in life.

The new souqs

For a decade the most famous souq in Sharjah was the 'New Souq', the double range of splendid vaulted buildings with their distinctive blue tile-work decoration, which is such a landmark on the northern shore of Khalid Lagoon, just opposite Jazira Park. Then in 1987 an equally splendid, even newer souq — the Souq Al Majarra — opened on the side of the creek and naming became a problem. In fact the New Souq is really called the Central Market, and perhaps one day it will be generally known as that too.

The New Souq (or Central Market) was designed by Michael Lyell Associates and won considerable acclaim when it was first opened in 1978. The identical parallel ranges of high barrel-vaulted buildings are linked by two flying bridges in the tradition of the 'Bridge of Sighs', and cooled by 10 high windtowers each. Inside they are extremely spacious, the high central alleyway rising right up into the roof, with two floors of little shops along each side. The whole complex houses 600 shops, 264 in each building and 36 on each bridge. Wide central stairways, and small stairs against the walls, give access to the upper floor which consists of a narrow passage running along the shop fronts and therefore has rather more of a souq atmosphere than the wide open lower floor.

Thus the upper floors in both buildings have developed more of a tourist appeal, with antique shops, carpet shops, a café and some traditional jewellery upstairs, while the ground floor in the section near the lagoon specialises in gold jewellery, perfumes, cassettes, videos and cameras. The UAE is one of the best markets in the world in which to buy gold jewellery, cassettes and electronic goods. In the other section of the souq the ground floor shops sell mostly ready-made clothes and shoes.

These large buildings are cooled by natural means only, yet seem always comfortable for the shopper. The breeze can blow right through the building, through the high entrance and pierced screens at either end, and these breezes

An elegant pinnacle on the New Souq stands outlined against the Khalid Lagoon, with the fountain rising high in the background.

are cooled by passing across pools of water and fountains at each end, and in the central opening of the buildings. Further breezes are successfully channelled downwards by the high wind-towers rising above the vaulted roofs.

The more recent modern souq, the Souq Al Majarra, which was designed by Halcrows and opened on the creekside in 1987, is closed at either end and cooled by air-conditioning. This souq also consists of a long, high building, this time with a great golden dome at its centre. This dome, a landmark on the creek front, has a diameter of 17

Kensington, London, and indeed the same stone that was used for that museum was also imported to Sharjah. The facade is hung with finely made, wrought-iron spherical lamps and decorated with little pinnacles at the roof line.

Along with the attractive, white building of the new souq in Khor Fakkan, cooled like the New Souq by high windtowers, these latter-day souqs are among the most distinguished buildings in the country. They offer shoppers a clean and comfortable environment in which to make their purchases, and the Sharjah New Souq

The Souq Al Majarra, on the creek front, is the most modern of Sharjah's souqs.

metres, and is specially treated to preserve it from heat and humidity.

Inside, the vast open space of the central alley-way rises to an arched ceiling. The shops are all on the ground floor and sell clothes, shoes and perfumes, and there is a café up above, under the dome which is decorated on the inside with a design of the night sky.

Outside, the Souq Al Majarra is a most handsome building, clad with a pink stone facing relieved by rows of blue-grey stone. The total effect is reminiscent of the Natural History Museum in

has become a great favourite of both tourists and foreign residents in search of traditional souvenirs and Persian carpets. They are, however, closer in atmosphere to rather grand shopping arcades than to the traditional souqs of the creekfront. There, the enclosed space created an intimate environment, conducive to conversation between shopper and shopkeeper, or among the old men gathered on the rickety benches in the narrow alleys; it was a sociable atmosphere which has not been recreated in the modern souqs, for all their splendour.

Inside Souq Al Majarra a high vaulted hall leads to an intricate entrance way.

Cultivation runs right up to the foot of golden sand dunes.

AGRICULTURE

There is a very fertile belt of land in the Emirate of Sharjah, on the gravel plain at the foot of the mountains, and especially along the skirts of the plain where the hard stony earth runs out under the encroaching sands. There, the greys and ochres of the desert landscape are slashed with patches of brilliant green — patches which spread and merge in the most favoured locations until they stretch uninterrupted for miles on end. There are places in Fili and Dhaid where it is hard to imagine oneself in Arabia at all.

Here some 3,700 farms have been developed, covering an area of 9,200 hectares. For the most part they draw their water from deep wells, continuously raised by motor-driven pumps. In the old palm groves of Dhaid and Fili, however, the water comes in part from a more unusual source. Both oases are fed by ancient falaj systems, water courses which run underground from the foot of the mountains, eventually coming to the surface among the palm trees. The very name of Fili is the local dialect pronunciation of falaj. The falaj of Dhaid was once one of the strongest in the country. It ran through the old mud fort which protected the oasis in the past, and surfaced just beyond the walls of the fort. Today the fort has been all but replaced by the modern police station, but the falaj runs beneath it still.

Despite the modern appearance of many of the farms, this was an area of very ancient cultivation. Dhaid was a key oasis at a cross road of trade routes, set beside a broad wadi which contributed to its generous water supplies. One former ruler in the past was prepared to accept this oasis as compensation for losing his emirate. A lone British surveying team in the early part of this century noted Dhaid Oasis as a potentially strategic staging post between the east and west coasts.

Crop from a Dhaid farm.

Picking the crop.

The nearby village of Mleiha stands near a site of even older import, that of a 2,000-year-old caravan town. One of the country's first experimental agricultural stations was established near Mleiha and today's farms overlie much of the site of the ancient town, drawing on exactly the same water resources.

Today's crops, however, far exceed anything that the inhabitants of those early farms could ever have known. In the past the oasis dweller concentrated essentially on the date palm which grew readily in poor soil and tolerated high salinity in the water. Each tree, properly cultivated, produced many kilos of dates every summer, valuable nourishment for both the cultivators and their animals. The extensive palm groves of Dhaid are still a witness to the former importance of this key crop. A few other crops were grown: barley and sorghum from very ancient times, limes, mangoes and alfalfa in more recent centuries.

A range of crops

Over the past few decades, however, an impressive range of crops has been introduced to the Emirates, and the selection is continually widening. Today most vegetables are growing well in the farms of Dhaid, Fili and Mleiha. Neat rows of cabbages, lettuce, beans, onions, carrots, squashes, aubergines, cucumbers, peppers, tomatoes and cauliflowers brighten the landscape, and fill the boxes to be carted off to market in the towns of the coast. Other farms are devoted to the cultivation of fruit trees. Here citrus fruits grow in profusion — oranges, lemons, grapefruit and pomelloes, a more original version of giant, slightly sweet grapefruit too. Limes of course, are still extremely successful, as are mangoes, guava and chico fruit. Some 64,000 tons of fruit and 27,000 tons of vegetables are produced each year in the Emirate of Sharjah. But the brightest green fields along the plain, those which often grow right up to the base of the dunes, usually turn out to be alfalfa, a kind of tall and luscious clover grown for animal fodder. Grass, maize and cattle beans are also grown to support the increasing number of herds in dairy farms, not to mention the hump-backed cattle of the villages and the cosseted racing camels along the edge of the dunes.

Farmers have had to come to terms with a whole range of enemies waiting to attack their precious crops. Insects, virus diseases, fungi and moulds can all decimate their production, invalidate a season's labours. Today, thanks largely to the efforts of experimental farms run by the Ministry of Agriculture, much is known about the problems in this region. The Ministry produces a series of useful leaflets on the cultivation of individual crops, and the eradication of pests and diseases. They provide subsidised insecticides, fertilisers, seeds and seedlings, and visit the farms of the region to offer advice and demonstration. Only careful cultivation will produce unflawed vegetables and fruit of a quality which can be sold in the home markets. For export, superior quality is even more essential.

Today many of the farmers use greenhouses ('plastika' as they are called locally) to assist their cultivation. The atmosphere inside these greenhouses can be controlled and they provide a sheltered, protected environment which is particularly suitable for young seedlings. Unlike in Europe, however, the farmers in Sharjah cool rather than heat their greenhouses. Fans extract the hot air while huge water-run desert coolers are set against the end walls. A moist atmosphere can be maintained by mist sprayed from above.

Inspecting cabbages for blight.

Fertilising chico trees.

Nursery garden at the strawberry farm.

'Emirates Strawberries' ripening at Mirak Farm near Dhaid.

The simplest greenhouses consist of metal hoops covered with plastic sheeting. These greenhouses are very effective but the thin plastic covers can be torn to shreds in high wind and the frequent replacement makes them expensive to maintain. In some farms the metal frames now support covers of black netting which are lowered in hot weather to provide shade for the crops.

Strawberries from Dhaid

One farm in Dhaid is diligently pioneering the production of 'Emirates Strawberries' which are beginning to make their mark in the supermarkets of the coastal towns, and even on world markets. The farmers realised that, while strawberries are common in the shops of Europe and the Far East in summer, they are not produced in those climes in winter. And it is precisely in winter that the strawberry can be grown in the UAE. So, in the mid-1980s, they began to grow their first strawberry plants.

They planted their strawberries on furrows, each mounded up and covered with black plastic sheeting to suppress any weeds or mould. This is a highly controlled environment, a far cry from picking among the nettles and thistles of so many strawberry fields in Europe. In the early years the farmers rapidly discovered the predators and diseases which could demolish their crops, and now can say with confidence that pests and diseases are under control. They soon found they could produce bumper harvests from January through to March or April. But excess crops for a short period were far less desirable than a more regular crop over a longer season, and this became the new challenge.

Each year new strawberry plants must be brought in from abroad since keeping them alive through the summer is not feasible. The company has experimented with different sources for their strawberry plants. The more mature the plants the quicker they will produce. This means they must buy from a cold country, where the new plants will be mature by the beginning of October. By autumn 1991, for instance, the farm was importing 700,000 plants by air from Canada. They stood the plants in a shaded nursery with mist spraying for a couple of weeks, to allow them to acclimatise and recover from the shock of the journey, then on October 1 they planted them out in the fields at night. All the planting was done by artificial lights in the dark, since it was still too hot by day.

Spraying crops under metal frames which can be shaded by netting in hot weather.

Within six weeks the first strawberries were ready for picking. The season had been extended back to mid-November, and would last now until early June. The heaviest crop is still in mid-winter, with an average of one-and-a-half tons of strawberries picked each day from early February to early May, but the load is becoming better spread each winter.

By 1990 the farm was producing 183 tons of strawberries per season, and increasing production

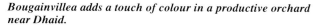

Bougainvillea adds a touch of colour in a productive orchard near Dhaid.

Many farmers supplement their diet by keeping a few pigeons on their land.

A small water cistern feeds irrigation channels.

substantially each year. The main markets are in the UAE, other Gulf countries, Holland, England, Hong Kong and Singapore. The farmers devoted eight hectares of their farm to strawberries and felt they could easily produce far more, but would have to make a major marketing effort abroad, to absorb the quickly perishable crop. The strawberries can be bought directly at the farm gate, on the road from Dhaid towards Masafi, at preferential prices throughout the winter.

This innovative farm is also experimenting with the introduction of new vegetables. They were the first to grow celery here, and with unusual ways of getting better crops from the current ones. In autumn, for instance, when their cold store is not needed for the harvested strawberries, they start their tomato seedlings in it, claiming to get stronger plants and heavier crops from seedlings which have come out from the cold.

Water resources

The strawberry farm is set well back from the palm groves of Dhaid, on the road towards the mountains. In that region the ground water resources are still plentiful and many new farms have been developed there. Further down the road towards the oasis, however, water supplies are running out and wells have to be sunk ever deeper. The danger then is that the deep water may be more saline than that from higher aquifers and can kill the crops. Today wells are being dug down to 1,000 or even 1,500 feet, and they do not always find water even at that depth. Happily the old palm groves are still doing well, since date palms are more tolerant of salt than most crops. Their falaj is kept running by having extra water pumped into it, but even so it has lost the strength of the olden days. Some newer farms have had to be abandoned altogether for lack of water.

A large new earthen dam has been constructed some 10 kilometres out of Dhaid, across the plain below the mountains. This vast and lengthy earthwork is intended not as a dam containing a reservoir behind it, but as a recharge dam. It should stop the wild run-off of flood water across the plain, holding it back long enough for the water to penetrate into the gravel layers below, whence it will flow underground towards the oasis. If there are good rains in future winters, this dam should help replenish the shallower aquifers, bringing abandoned wells and derelict farms back to life again.

Bringing in the alfalfa crop grown in fields at the foot of the dunes.

Excavations at Mleiha of houses over 2,000 years old.

AN ANCIENT PAST

Sharjah Creek was clearly an attractive site for a settlement, from the very earliest days of human habitation along the coastline. It offered a safe harbour for small boats, and the shallow tidal lagoons inland of the creek were rich in fish and shellfish, basic elements of the diet in olden days. So, on the line of sand dunes around the flat, coastal basin, the debris of settlements some 6,000 years old has been found. Piles of seashells lay mixed with chips of shiny flint, with a few beautiful flint arrowheads and knives among them. A particularly fine collection of such flint tools was discovered on the sandy rise in Abu-Shagharah and another in Al Yarmuk.

A caravan city

Some time later, the centre of activity in the Emirate of Sharjah shifted inland. A substantial town was developed on the caravan route running across the country from the east to west coasts. There, at the foot of the mountains, a wealthy trading town grew up near Mleiha, at the base of Jebel Faya. The site was inhabited for nearly a thousand years, from 600 BC or earlier. The town flourished from about 200 BC until nearly 200 AD. It lies in an area which today has been developed as fertile farmland. The water table below the plain was plentiful and this must have been the attraction of the site.

The ancient town of Mleiha is particularly important in the history of the UAE since inscriptions in several different languages and scripts have been found there; indeed Mleiha has provided almost all of the ancient writings found anywhere in the UAE. Most exciting perhaps are tombstones written in ancient south Arabian script, probably by settlers coming from the southern or eastern

Tombstone with South Arabian writing, which was found at Mleiha. (Photo: Remy Boucharlat)

This Roman-style statue was unearthed by a farmer in Mleiha. (Photo: Remy Boucharlat)

region of Saudi Arabia. They are a clear sign that Arabs had arrived in the UAE by the 2nd century BC, more than 2,000 years ago.

Then there are inscriptions on bronze bowls in south Arabian script, and plaques written in Aramaic, the language of northern Arabia. Fragments of fine bowls show pictures in relief of camel and horse-riders and of lions, and one bears the word 'Mara'shams', a reference perhaps to the sun deity 'Shams'. The bowl was probably made in the 3rd century BC.

From almost as early a time are half-a-dozen amphorae handles, stamped in Greek with the name of the makers from the island of Rhodes. They show that Mleiha's trade links spread from the Mediterranean, through northern and eastern Arabia, and as far south as the Yemen from whence incense and perfumes were imported.

French archaeologists have uncovered the remains of substantial mud-brick houses. Indeed, the whitish outlines of ancient walls can still be seen running across much of the desert between the farms. They have also excavated two impressive cemeteries, whose graves were cut down into large pits in the desert floor. The tombs were then roofed over and tall towers built above them. These towers must have stood three to four metres high and were built of hard white bricks, with white-brick crowstep crenellations around the tops of them. Great quantities of iron weapons — arrowheads, daggers and swords — were found in the tombs, along with fine little alabaster jars. These tiny jars, with crouching animals modelled on their lids, came from southern Arabia and contained perfumes.

Small alabaster perfume jar. (Photo: Remy Boucharlat)

The fine new museum on the 'Culture Roundabout'.

Finds from the excavations are displayed in the new museum in Sharjah being completed in 1992. This elegant museum has a lofty entrance hall with models of Sharjah in 1932 and of Al Khan; exhibition rooms on two storeys display objects from Sharjah's past. The most modern methods of temperature and humidity control are installed and there are laboratories for cleaning and conservation of ancient objects.

Sharjah itself may also have existed as a town at this time. An ancient map, drawn up in the 2nd century AD by the Greek geographer Ptolemy from Alexandria, marks a stretch of coastline which seems to be the UAE. This shows a large wadi, probably Wadi Lamhah which flows through Dhaid and Falaj Al Mualla, to reach the sea between Umm Al Quwain and Ras Al Khaimah. To the south-west of it are marked places named Cauana and Sarcoa, names still close enough to Quwain and Sharjah to be perhaps recognisable even after nearly two millennia.

Attractive little model of a typical traditional village, on display in the museum.

A PROUD HISTORY

Sharjah is recorded as early as 1490 AD by the great Arab navigator, Ahmad ibn Majid, who describes in one of his nautical manuals a journey around this coastline, and mentions Sharjah, Umm Al Quwain and Ras Al Khaimah:

*'The stars will guide you to Tunb, summer and winter,
And they show the true way from Tunb to Sharjah.'*

Europeans sail into the Gulf

Ahmad ibn Majid was a well-known seafarer when the Portuguese admiral, Vasco da Gama, was seeking to extend Portuguese trade with the East. The Portuguese soon realised the richness of the spice trade, and sought to establish their control of all the harbours along the route. One of the very best harbours on the east coast of Arabia is that of Khor Fakkan and in 1507 it fell prey to the Portuguese commander Alfonso de Albuquerque. The town was bravely defended by horse-riders who rode down onto the beach to do battle with the invaders, but they were over-whelmed. The young men were taken off to work in the galleys of the Portuguese ships, while the old men were left mutilated, their noses and ears cut off.

With such methods the Portuguese soon estab-lished their hold of the east coast and built a number of forts by which to control it. They had forts in Kalba, Khor Fakkan and Dibba, all now Sharjah territory, and left plans and descriptions of the buildings they erected. They ruled the coast-line for a little more than a century, and used Khor Fakkan as a supply port. Its waters were the sweetest in all Arabia, they recorded, and gardens and palm groves there ensured a supply of dates, limes and oranges. Today nothing is to

Dibba's ancient fort was converted into a police station.

Khor Fakkan impressed the Portuguese as 'a very big place'.

be seen of the Portuguese fort at Khor Fakkan, though a mound and ruined towers near the creek of Khor Kalba, and remains of the old fort of Dibba, may mark the sites of those other forts.

When Portuguese power in the Gulf waned, they were replaced for a while by the Dutch, who were also building a great far eastern trade. A Dutchman, Van Kniphausen, wrote a description of the Gulf coasts in 1755 with the following note on UAE territory (where Abu Dhabi and Dubai had not yet been founded): 'Between Catif and Zur, along the coast, there are three places, Aseer, Guhar (Julfar) and Scharge (Sharjah). These places consist of only a few houses each, where dates and rice are brought from Bassora, to sell to the Arabs of the desert and to the pearl divers.'

Pearl diving was a basic occupation in the Gulf, alongside maritime trade. It had certainly attracted the Portuguese who had recorded two centuries earlier: 'Passing above this place Profam (Khor Fakkan) we come to another called Julfar, where dwell persons of great wealth, great navigators and wholesale dealers. Here is a very great fishery as well of seed pearls as of large pearls. . . ' Then, as now, the fortunes of coastal towns ebbed and flowed; as the centuries passed, they prospered and expanded, or shrank and became villages.

For hundreds, perhaps thousands of years, pearl diving was a major source of their prosperity. Until the 1930s great pearling fleets went out from each of the harbours to the pearling banks each summer, in the arduous quest for fine pearls of which the Gulf was the world's main supplier. But in the 1930s the Japanese developed the cultured pearl and the market for natural pearls collapsed. The crash of the pearl trade marked the saddest ebb of all in the fortunes of the Emirates, a low point in which, fortunately, the discovery of oil came as a welcome relief.

British in the Gulf

The Portuguese and Dutch were followed along the route to the East by the British, an emerging maritime power intent on developing their trade links with India. The Gulf, along with the Red Sea passage, was one of the principal routes of communication favoured by the European powers between the Mediterranean and India and by the 18th century shipping was active there. By the early part of the 17th century the British East India Company had established a trading factory at

Detail from the 1669 map shown on page 78. Quiximi (Qasimi) is marked approximately where Sharjah is.

Gombroon (Bandar Abbas) and it was here that the British came across another rising naval power of the Gulf, the Qawasim, who were also keen to participate in the trade of the region and to enhance their long-standing markets in India.

The British and the Qawasim sailed the waters of the Gulf and Arabian Sea harmoniously together for the rest of the century. Francis Warden, the Secretary to the Government of Bombay which had responsibility for the region, wrote, 'From the period of their establishment in Oman until the year 1796, I have been unable to trace a single act of aggression, even on the part of the Joasmees (Qawasim), against the British flag.' Throughout this period the Qawasim rapidly became the dominant local maritime power of the region. From their strongholds in Ras Al Khaimah and Sharjah they established their authority over a number of islands and ports on both sides of the Gulf, most noticeably Qishm and Lingeh (which they held until the early 20th century). J S Buckingham, a British traveller and writer of the time, explained the success of the Qawasim thus: 'All (of the Qawasim), however, were so much more skilful, industrious and faithful in their engagements (dealings) than the other tribes of the coast, that they were always preferred and constantly spoken of as the best people throughout the Gulf.'

However, around the turn of the century, relations between the Qawasim and the British deteriorated. The British, having by then established their dominion over much of India, gave preference to their own vessels and those of Indian ships sailing under their protection in the markets of the subcontinent to the detriment of other traders. In return for naval facilities at Muscat, which greatly assisted the defence of their Indian territories against a perceived threat from the French and Russians, the British gave political support to the Sultan of Muscat who, for much of the latter part of the 18th century, had been in competition with the Qawasim for dominance in the region.

The British blamed all attacks on their shipping on the Qawasim. In his well documented book *The Myth of Arab Piracy in the Gulf,* HH Dr Sheikh Sultan bin Mohammed Al Qasimi has shown there are two sides to the story, questioning the validity of reports given at the time and showing the Joasmees were often blamed for others' misdemeanours.

By 1809, relations between the British and the Qawasim had deteriorated to such a level

Scene of the British attack on Ras Al Khaimah on
13 November, 1809 from a painting by R Temple.

that, when an army and naval support became available in Bombay, the Government of the East India Company needed little persuasion to mount an expedition against the Qawasim. Thus in November, 1809, Ras Al Khaimah and other towns belonging to the Joasmees on the Arabian side of the Gulf were attacked and burned together with their ships. Lingeh and Qishm on the other side of the Gulf suffered a similar fate.

Soon, however, the industrious Qawasim had rebuilt their towns and an even bigger fleet. British complaints were renewed. Sensing danger, Sheikh Hassan bin Rahma Al Qasimi, Chieftan of Ras Al Khaimah, made earnest attempts to maintain peace with the British through their Resident at Bushire, the Governor of Bombay and by the mediation of Sheikh Abdullah bin Ahmad, Chieftan of Bahrain. Whilst maintaining his efforts for peace, Hassan bin Rahma Al Qasimi tried to forge a defensive alliance between the tribes of the Gulf against a potential threat by the British.

The formation of such an alliance, including the great Sheikh of the Qawasim, Sultan bin Saqr, must have further alarmed the British and in 1819, with Omani help, they resolved to destroy the power of the Qawasim once and for all. In November of that year they again attacked and destroyed the Qasimi strongholds along both shores of the Gulf together with their fleets. A general Treaty of Peace was signed in 1820 between the British and the Sheikhs of the coastal towns which guaranteed peace at sea, and the protection of the British against external aggression for 150 years. Further truces were signed later between the British and the ruling Sheikhs giving birth to the country known as the Trucial States.

Sultan bin Saqr and his sons

Although Sheikh Sultan bin Saqr, who had become Ruler of the Qawasim in 1803, had begun his rule so traumatically, he was destined to have a long and fortunate reign over the Qawasim. He ruled for over half-a-century until his death at the age of 86, in 1866; he governed the extensive Qawasim domains with the help first of his brothers and then of his sons. He himself made his headquarters in Sharjah, but sometimes he moved to Ras Al Khaimah, Lingeh or Qishm island.

Yesterday's watchtowers are simply monuments to the past for today's youth.

A fine old watchtower, which once guarded Sharjah's northern approaches, still stands in the Abu Shagharah district.

By the middle of the century he finally managed to establish definitively his rule over the east coast of his domains. This was formally recognised in an agreement of 1850 with the Sultan of Muscat, who ceded to the Qawasim all territories north of a line from Khor Kalba to Sharjah and south of a line from Dibba to Sha'am.

Sadly, towards the end of Sheikh Sultan's life, two of his sons died in battle, one helping to suppress a rebellion at Hamriya, and another in single combat (shades of early Greek and Roman history) against the Sheikh of Abu Dhabi. Several sons survived him, however, and they and his grandsons were to rule in Sharjah and Ras Al Khaimah until well into the 20th century, when the rule passed to his great grandsons and to his great great grandson. After so long and strong a rule, it was not easy for his immediate descendants to hold Sheikh Sultan bin Saqr's domains together. Over the following century various sections of the Qawasim territory sought independence from central rule and eventually both Ras Al Khaimah and Fujairah became independent Emirates, recognised by the British in 1921 and 1952 respectively.

The old fort which was once the airport resthouse.

The control tower of the UAE's first airport.

The Sharjah Continental Hotel now dominates the once-fickle entrance to the creek.

The leading Emirate

Sharjah remained, however, the leading town in the country. In the 19th century it was described as the second most important port in the whole Gulf, following only after Kuwait. In recognition of Sharjah's primary position, the British established a political representative there in 1823. This was to remain their only diplomatic agency in the whole of the Emirates (the Trucial States then) for well over a hundred years, until a political agency was opened in Dubai in 1954.

At the beginning of the 20th century the Gulf received a visit steeped in pomp and circumstance. Lord Curzon, Viceroy of India, toured the region with his fleet in 1903, stopping to hold magnificent receptions — known as Durbars — at the major ports. For the Trucial States he naturally chose Sharjah for his Durbar and his ships anchored some distance offshore. The deck of his cruiser, the Argonaut, was transformed into a splendid pavilion, ablaze with rich hangings, gold embroidered carpets, elegant chairs, and the flags of many nations. The Sheikhs of Sharjah, Abu Dhabi, and Dubai came with their sons, along with the Sheikh of Ajman and the son of the ailing Ruler of Umm Al Quwain. Their 'dignified and independent air and the manly appearance of their followers occasioned general remark', it was recorded. In his speech Lord Curzon remarked that all were aware that the east coast was "under the Chief of the Jowasmis. Nevertheless his authority is contested in some quarters. It is desirable that these disputes should cease, and that the peace should remain undisturbed." Since it was the month of Ramadhan no refreshments were served (fortunate perhaps as the sea was very rough), but gifts of guns, swords and gold watches were offered to the Sheikhs before they left for home.

Some 30 years later, Sharjah became the first place in the Emirates to have an airport. Imperial Airways, forerunners of British Airways, were seeking landing facilities on the route to India. Sheikh Sultan of Sharjah agreed that they could construct an airstrip near his town, provided the mail steamer to India should call at Sharjah too. In return the British authorities were to pay him rent and landing fees, and gave a promise that Sharjah territory should remain intact.

In 1932 a landing strip was built close to the town, running due east from the present-day King Faisal Mosque. The old runway has now become a

The husn, the Ruler's fort-cum-palace, which stood on the site of Al Burj Avenue until the 1960s.

wide road called King Abdul Aziz Street. The old control tower still stands on vacant land there, close beside a large fort-like building which was the original resthouse for the airport.

Four years later, the British were seeking emergency landing rights on the east coast also. They negotiated a deal with Kalba which gave that small town independence from Sharjah, as a separate Emirate, in return for the use of an airstrip there. Kalba was to remain independent, ruled by another branch of the Qasimi family, from 1936 until 1951 when it was finally reabsorbed into the Emirate of Sharjah.

The airport at Sharjah brought a welcome additional income to the Emirate at a time when the pearl trade, one of the major sources of income for the country as a whole, was facing disaster. By the 1940s the annual expedition of the pearling fleets to the oyster banks had virtually ceased. But by this time Sharjah acquired new sources of income and importance, for it became a base for the RAF, and soon afterwards the headquarters

of the country's newly-formed local forces, the Trucial Oman Scouts. By 1937 a British political officer spent the cool months of the year in Sharjah, and in 1948 a permanent British political officer was stationed there, responsible for the country as a whole. In 1953 the first modern school was opened in Sharjah and attracted sons of leading families from neighbouring emirates.

At this time, however, Sharjah's fortunes lapsed again. The sand bar dividing her creek from the sea crept inexorably across the opening of the creek, until it became impossible for shipping to enter. Dubai's creek was also silting as a result of the same currents, but just stayed open long enough to be rescued by modern technology in the mid-1950s. So shipping to the area moved across to Dubai, whose trade flourished as a result. In 1954 the British moved their representative to Dubai which became the centre of activity for the next decade, until the discovery of great quantities of oil in Abu Dhabi shifted the centre once more towards the south-west.

Within the UAE

Under the leadership of her former Ruler, Sheikh Khalid bin Mohammed Al Qasimi, Sharjah joined the UAE at its formation in December 1971. Sharjah was to play an active role in the federation, and in recognition of her long experience of modern education has provided the Minister of Education ever since. Shortly after the founding of the UAE, however, following the untimely death of Sheikh Khalid, his younger brother, Sheikh Sultan bin Mohammed, was chosen as Ruler.

He has led the Emirate throughout the period of very rapid development which has succeeded the founding of the UAE and the discovery of oil in Sharjah territory. Sheikh Sultan was to become Sharjah's scholar Sheikh. He was already well-educated with a degree in agriculture when he became Ruler, and he has continued to extend and deepen his studies ever since. In 1985 he obtained a doctorate in history from the University of Exeter, and he has since then published a number of extensively documented books on the history of the area, in both English and Arabic.

During the past few decades the city of Sharjah has expanded beyond recognition. Its population in 1959 was estimated at 5,000; in the census of 1985 the population of the Emirate, most of whom live in Sharjah town, was put at 269,000, and numbers have continued to increase since then.

Development of the Emirate as a whole has also continued apace, most especially with the construction of modern highways linking all corners of Sharjah territory, and bringing in particular easy access to the towns of the east coast. Until the 1970s, access to the east coast was a slow and difficult undertaking, for 4WD vehicles only, taking rough tracks through the wadis and over the mountains.

Today some of these wadi tracks still exist, to the great delight of tourists and picnickers, but the main road to the east coast is smooth and rapid, and takes little more than an hour from the centre of Sharjah city.

The towns of Sharjah and Khor Fakkan are expanding rapidly and new industrial ventures are actively encouraged. Peace, and with it prosperity, in the Gulf is proving as great a benefit to Sharjah's economy as it is to those of other states throughout the region.

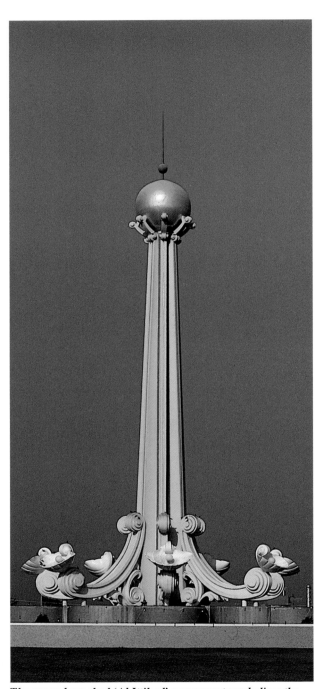

The seven-branched 'Al Ittihad' monument symbolises the Federation of the seven emirates in the United Arab Emirates.

HH Dr Sheikh Sultan bin Mohammed Al Qasimi, Member of the Supreme Council and Ruler of Sharjah, presenting prizes to outstanding students.

Modern highways now link all corners of the Emirate of Sharjah.

The East Coast offers magnificent beaches and excellent water sports, centred on the Oceanic Hotel at Khor Fakkan.

LEISURE AND SPORTS

The warm winter sunshine of the Gulf region makes sport and outdoor activities of all kinds a powerful attraction, even for the most unsporty of individuals. Residents and holiday-makers alike are tempted to try their hand at sports they never dreamed of tackling, and for those who really balk at launching out, there are exciting 'spectator sports' to get them out of doors.

Winter and summer alike, water sports are likely to top anyone's list. This is even more true in summer, when the sea becomes so warm that one can happily spend all day in the water, and pools are cooled for a more energetic swim. For water sports Sharjah is uniquely well placed since it includes along its sandy Gulf coast three fine, sheltered creeks which offer safe havens for a wide range of activities. And then, on the east coast, an even wider range of sea sports is available; here clear blue seas, with rocky cliffs dropping steeply into the water, harbour a kaleidoscopic array of colourful tropical fish, elegant corals and other picturesque sea creatures like the Crown of Thorns starfish, sea urchins, cowries and other attractive shellfish.

At the Oceanic Hotel in Khor Fakkan scuba diving courses are available and diving expeditions are organised to explore the riches of this rocky east coast. Fishing excursions are also available from this hotel, outings which may bring in a haul of tasty hamour, red snapper or kingfish. While the 'armchair fisherman' may merely be content with watching a team of local fishermen laboriously hauling in their seine nets on the beach, one of the most photogenic scenes in the whole Emirate. If he is fortunate, when the catch is finally pulled in, he may be given a bagful of sparkling sardines to grill there and then over charcoal on the seashore.

Beach sports at Khor Fakkan.

Baby camels roam the desert in spring.

Mountain wadis offer exciting safaris. (Photo: Orient Tours)

In the creeks on the west coast sea sports are more energetic, and perhaps yet more amusing for the onlookers. In the picturesque creek of Al Khan, sweeping round behind the old village on its promontory of sand, or the wide Khalid Lagoon in Sharjah town, or yet again in the long Hamriyah Creek to the north of Ajman, the most recent craze in water sports always takes precedence. For a while water-skiing boats were predominant, then windsurfers swept the field (or rather the waters) while today jetskis chase in and out of the mouth of the creeks. These diminutive but rapid craft are at their most exciting, in the hands of a strong sportsman, cresting the waves of a rough sea. But for the family user, the safe waters of the creek are the ideal location both for jetskis and windsurfs.

Creeks and beaches are also ideal for more gentle exercise, bathing, sunbathing and simply pottering in the sun. Sharjah's leading hotels are all sited either on the beach, the creek or the lagoon, and each of them has a sweet water swimming pool alongside the salt water of the sea. There are also more remote beaches, for a picnic away from the crowds, such as the public beach now equipped with thatched sunshades and planted with a fringe of young palm trees, between Sharjah and Ajman. And the long, unspoilt beach running beneath a steep sand dune, to the north of Hamriyah.

Desert excursions

Sand dunes indeed, are an attraction in themselves. Sharjah has some of the most picturesque sand desert in the UAE, running inland in great billows of sand from the west coast. Here there are areas of pure dunes, like the challenging sands near Mleiha which are so popular with dune drivers. The great sand slide, from the top of Jebel Mleiha, offers the ultimate in excitement to dune drivers. And then there are other regions where the dunes are clad with coppices of weeping ghaf trees, offering welcome shade for a picnic in the sands.

Sharjah's 'Orient Tours' were first in the UAE to exploit this sandy wonderland, offering outings and barbecues in the desert, with experienced sand drivers as guides. They, and Sharjah's other tour operators, also take visitors up into the mountain wadis where a bumpy drive over rocky tracks can bring you to a hidden oasis of date palms and clear pools of crystal mountain water. Or for the more adventurous, 4WD vehicles can

The beauty of the desert can best be experienced through an excursion by 4WD.

be hired by the day from any of the car hire firms, though one should never go alone into the sands; always arrange to go with at least one, and preferably two other cars. Even the experts can easily become stuck in the sands, and often the only way out is a tow from another vehicle.

One of the attractions of the desert is always the people and animals who manage to make their lives in such a taxing environment. How, one wonders, can anything survive in a landscape so stripped of surface adornment. Foremost among the great survivors of the desert are the camels which happily still roam in great numbers in the sands. In springtime the baby camels will be the most photographed of desert denizens, while throughout the winter the strings of racing camels in brightly coloured blankets, trekking to and fro from one camel race track to another, add their own special touch of colour to the ochre landscape.

Camel races are held on Thursdays and Fridays during the winter at a race track among the red sands near Dhaid. Race weekends alternate between the tracks of Dhaid, Umm Al Quwain and Ras Al Khaimah, so it is well to check in advance where the races will be on any given weekend. The scene is a colourful one, with tiny jockeys in brightly coloured racing shirts and caps, perched on their huge mounts, urging them on with little sticks when the word comes over the walkie-talkies in their breast pockets, from the trainers racing alongside the track in their 4WDs. Jockeys and mounts are delighted to be photographed, as are many of the trainers too. Camel racing, or rather sale of the winning camels, allows large sums of money to circulate among the Bedouin of the desert and is a sport which has gained greatly in popularity throughout the UAE in recent years.

Windsurfer on the safe and sheltered water of Hamriyah Creek.

Sports

Coming back towards Sharjah town from the camel races at Dhaid, one passes the Sharjah Equestrian Club, also out in the sands. Here horse races and other competitions are held, and there is the possiblility also of a quiet trip out into the sand dunes.

Yet another 'desert' sport, nearby along the same road, is provided by the Sharjah golf course. Here the fairways are dunes and the greens are 'browns' — firm circles of sand compacted with oil. For winter days it provides pleasant sport, while the real golf enthusiast can find expensively grassed golf courses some 20 kilometres away, in the neighbouring Emirate of Dubai.

In fact just about all western sports are available in Sharjah and most of them can be played all year round. Even in summer, when the temperatures rise to great heights by day, tennis courts and football pitches are floodlit at night and the exercise they offer in the evenings and early mornings provides a welcome break from the still of the day.

Among the sports offered by the hotels are tennis, with coaching available, squash, gymnasia and bowling alleys. Most of the hotels also have

windsurfs, other boating facilities and heat-regulated swimming pools.

The leading sports club for western-style sports is the Sharjah Wanderers, an active well-equipped club which is a hive of activity, especially at the weekend during the cooler season. This club runs hockey, rugby, soccer, tennis, squash and darts teams and has a swimming pool and restaurant for family days out.

The Marbella Club, on the shores of the Khalid Lagoon, is another social and sports club right in the heart of the city. This club offers all kinds of water sports, as well as tennis, squash, snooker, darts, mini-golf and a gymnasium. Its white, domed chalets set in a garden environment are reminiscent of the atmosphere of its Spanish namesake.

Sharjah cricket

Quite surprisingly, the sport for which Sharjah has won international renown is cricket. The world's top cricket teams gather twice a year for a week-long, hard-fought tournament in the city's fine cricket stadium where they play before large and enthusiastic audiences, many of them from the cricketers' home countries. Cricket in Sharjah is the creation of Abdulrahman Bukhatir, a Sharjah businessman whose boyhood dream — fostered by schooling in the Indian subcontinent — was always of top class cricket. He built the fine stadium in 1981, and ever since has organised the now world-famous Cricketers' Benefit Fund Series of tournaments at which the national teams of all the leading cricket-playing nations in the world have participated.

At the end of the matches, organised in a series of day-long games in which each side bats for 50 overs, or half-a-day, the winning team and selected outstanding players all receive a generous purse. Some of the great old men of cricket are also invited along, to receive a purse of their own at the farewell party.

Teams from Pakistan, Bangladesh, India, Sri Lanka, Australia, New Zealand, Great Britain and the West Indies are all familiar to Sharjah. And in autumn 1991 the International Cricket Council met there to take the welcome decision to include once again the South African team in world cricket. So Sharjah was able to be the first to invite South Africa to attend tournaments in future.

On a quieter note Sharjah has become one of the leading centres for chess in the UAE. Chess

International cricketers enjoying a refreshment break at Sharjah's stadium.

The Marbella features an Arab-Andalusian style 'village'.

clubs for both men and women attract talented boys and girls who will one day be representing their country in this sport in which the Emirates is already carving itself a name.

Nightlife

So much sport, even if only savoured as a spectator, is likely to produce a healthy appetite which Sharjah's hotels and restaurants are well-equipped to meet. The major hotels have restaurants offering top international cuisine, with specialities from all around the world. They produce a wide and delicious range of fruit juice cocktails and other non-alcoholic drinks. Sharjah's hotels follow the general UAE rule for restaurants outside hotels, and do not serve alcohol.

There are also many ordinary restaurants which serve excellent food at very reasonable prices. Some of these restaurants have created an interesting and original atmosphere of their own, especially those sited around the Khalid Lagoon. Here, there is a dhow restaurant set in a converted wooden boat, a café run in a traditional palm-frond hut on the banks of the Lagoon, and a Lebanese restaurant whose terrace overhangs the water. Close by is the Marbella Club restaurant, with gardens running down to the Lagoon.

The individual hotels organise evening entertainment, dancing and variety shows as well as 'special events' weeks. International theatre groups perform in the fine Cultural Centre.

The Oceanic is nestled among the dramatic Hajar Mountains.

The Al Gargour Rooftop Restaurant offers plush dining facilities.

The diving centre is staffed by professional instructors.

SHARJAH HOTELS

The Oceanic Hotel

Khor Fakkan, about one-and-a-half hours' drive from the city centres of Dubai and Sharjah, boasts of one of the finest beach resorts on the East Coast. Nestled among the dramatic Hajar Mountains, overlooking the azure waters of the Indian Ocean, is the Oceanic Hotel.

Relax to the gentle sound of the surf; sunbathe on the unspoilt expanse of private beach; swim in the clear warm ocean waters; take a dive in the hotel's fresh-water pool, or a sunset cruise around the bay.

The Oceanic offers de luxe comfort with its 162 air-conditioned luxury rooms and suites, each one with its Italian cream-veined marble bathroom. All rooms and suites have direct-dial telephones, national television channels, in-house cable TV, 4-channel piped music, a mini fridge and 24-hour room service.

Guests can enjoy Continental, Arabic, Chinese or Indian cuisine and a vast array of fresh sea food. The Al Murjan overlooks the private beach while the Al Gargour Rooftop Restaurant and Lounge provides a breathtaking view of Khor Fakkan Bay.

The Blue Bay Pool has a special separate pool for toddlers. The Al Rolla Banquet Hall is the ideal setting for large parties or business conventions and a complete range of audio visual equipment is available.

The Health and Fitness Centre offers ultra-modern equipment for a work-out. The hotel has a wide range of water and sea sports and a professionally-equipped diving centre. Diving trips are conducted by professional PADI diving instructors and this vicinity provides one of the best spots in the UAE for underwater exploration. Its flood-lit tennis courts are designed to international standards.

The hotel has a range of watersports facilities.

Hotel Holiday International

Situated at the edge of Sharjah's picturesque Khalid Lagoon, Hotel Holiday International is barely 20 minutes away from Dubai and Sharjah airports. Its central location offers guests easy access to Sharjah's souq, the International Expo Centre and the scenic Corniche.

This luxurious complex offers 255 spacious rooms and suites with individually controlled room temperature and air-conditioning. Each room, with a balcony, offers a beautiful view of Sharjah and has a fully equipped private bathroom, queen-size bed, radio, colour television, in-house movies showing the latest Arabic and English films, mini bar, direct-dial telephone and 24-hour room service.

The hotel offers a host of facilities including seven-day transit visa arrangements, valet and laundry services, an executive business bureau and travel agency, safety deposit boxes, mail and postage and car rentals.

The Al Majlis Conference Hall which affords a breathtaking view from the rooftop, can accommodate up to 60 people. It is fully equipped with state-of-the-art audio and video equipment and is ideal for boardroom meetings, corporate presentations, company seminars, private dinners and receptions.

Al Dana, one of the largest ballrooms and banquet halls in the UAE, is also equipped to host conferences, seminars, large banquets, fashion shows, weddings and even automobile and electronic expositions for up to 1,000 people. Four built-in partitions can provide syndicate rooms, each with a capacity of 250 people.

The Tea Garden offers round-the-clock service.

A sumptuous spread is laid out in the Oasis Restaurant.

The spacious Presidential Suite is luxuriously fitted.

The hotel's rooftop restaurant Al Kasr, offers a panoramic view of the city and special Theme Nights with live entertainment. The Oasis Restaurant extends all the way down to the pool and the live entertainment enhances the casual atmosphere. Delicious international cuisine is served à la carte but if guests prefer, they can partake of breakfast, lunch and dinner buffets.

The Tea Garden, an airy, friendly lobby restaurant serves a variety of light meals and snacks round-the-clock and is noted for its quick service. Evenings here provide a cosy, relaxed atmosphere with special live entertainment.

For the more adventurous, there is The Saloon with its Wild West ambience, complete with a Tex-Mex atmosphere, live entertainment and an exciting range of Mexican, Texan and 'Wild-Ranch' cuisine.

Set amidst lush gardens, the Pool Snack Bar offers everything from snacks to full meals.

The hotel's temperature-controlled swimming pool has a sun terrace and children's pool. Other sports and recreational facilities include a gymnasium, a children's playground, a range of watersports and indoor games.

The gym in the Holiday Club is fully equipped.

One of the Club's two swimming pools.

Marbella Club

Sporting an Arab-Andalusian ambience, the Marbella Club offers first-class hotel facilities. Surrounded by exotic gardens on the edge of the Khalid Lagoon, it combines a high standard of quality with a spirit of hospitality and personal attention.

Located on the Corniche Road, it is situated in the heart of the city. The New Souq which lies a short walk from the Marbella is one of the architectural wonders of the Middle East.

This miniature 'village' comprises villas, junior and master suites — all tastefully decorated with a private bathroom, air-conditioning, direct-dialling facilities, radio, colour television, in-house movies and room service.

There is a variety of cuisine at the Marbella Club — Italian, Arabic, Indian and Continental for private functions, indoor and outdoor catering. The Italian Restaurant, with its beautiful land-scaped garden setting and its authentic food and architecture provides a romantic aura. Adjoining the restaurant is a Pizzeria with a traditional Italian oven which burns firewood. Pizza take-aways are available on request.

The Marbella Club's attractive chalets are set in gardens running down to the Khalid Lagoon. (Courtesy of the Department of Information)

The accommodation is cosy and equipped with modern amenities.

Caesar's Palace serves authentic Italian food.

The Rendezvous Coffee Shop, near the pool, serves breakfast, lunch and afternoon tea with delicious crêpes and pastries. In the evenings there is a fine selection of seafood — exotic shellfish and fresh fish specially prepared to order.

The Club has a host of sports facilities including fully equipped fishing boat trips, waterskiing, windsurfing, sailing, two flood-lit tennis courts, air-conditioned squash courts, two swimming pools and a children's play area. In addition, the Club offers ballet, karate, yoga, jazz exercise, ballroom and international dance classes supervised by qualified professional teachers.

Guests can also visit the hairdressing salon, the perfume shop and the unique Belgium Chocolate Shop.

The Sharjah Carlton Hotel is surrounded by colourful gardens.

The Al Atlal Restaurant and Coffee Shop offers a varied selection of cuisine.

Sharjah Carlton Hotel

A mere five kilometres from Sharjah city centre, stands the Sharjah Carlton Hotel, a beach-front property surrounded by a wide expanse of colourful gardens. Not far from the hotel is the picturesque traditional village of Al Khan with its watchtower on the beach. In front are the warm waters of the Arabian Gulf.

The Sharjah Carlton is a full facility de luxe hotel, rich in oriental tradition. The beautifully designed and furnished Royal Suites have an attached private lounge and two balconies. The luxurious, cosy atmosphere is enhanced by modern amenities. The refurbished spacious rooms are also equipped with a private bathroom, mini fridge, direct-dial telephone, colour television, video in-house movie channel and radio.

The bungalows, offering the same room facilities, lie adjacent to the hotel and have direct access to the swimming pools and the private beach. Single, double and twin accommodation is available on request.

To facilitate guests, the hotel also handles visa requirements, reservations and onward bookings, a courtesy airport service and shuttle bus service to Dubai and Sharjah city centres. And for the businessman, there is a fully equipped secretarial, facsimile, telex and courier service.

Other facilities include a valet service, a salon for ladies and gentlemen, a books and gift shop, express laundry on request and a rent-a-car and taxi service.

The Al Mubarakia Hall offers a complete range of conference and banqueting facilities and can accommodate up to 600 people. The Al Atlal Restaurant and Coffee Shop provides a wide selection of Continental, Oriental and European cuisine, with an array of à la carte specialities and lavish luncheon buffets and dinners. For utmost convenience and privacy, guests are provided with a 24-hour room service.

The Health Club and Fitness Centre has a gymnasium, massage parlour, steam bath and sauna. In the Amusement Room, indoor sports enthusiasts can indulge in billiards and table tennis.

The range of sports and leisure facilities includes two large temperature-controlled swimming pools, a flood-lit tennis court and a private beach with soft silver sands and sparkling blue waters. The charming tropical Beach Café serves savoury snacks and refreshments.

The well-appointed rooms are spacious and relaxing.

The hotel's private beach and range of sports facilities attract guests.

The hotel's private beach is a favourite with guests.

Sharjah Continental Hotel

Dominating the entrance to Sharjah harbour, and with its own private and secluded beach, stands the Sharjah Continental Hotel, a five-star property built to international standards. Opened in 1982 by the Ruler of Sharjah, HH Dr Sheikh Sultan bin Mohammed Al Qasimi, its distinctive architecture makes it a special landmark.

It lies near the commercial centre and the New Souq. It has easy access to the airports of Sharjah and Dubai. For the convenience of guests, the hotel runs a regular bus shuttle to Sharjah city and Dubai. Car rental and a de luxe limousine service are also available, catering to the tourist, businessman and conference delegate alike.

A 150-foot atrium window looks down on a spacious lobby sporting a glorious garden with palm trees and a waterfall. To add to the romantic setting are birds which are allowed to fly around freely. This provides the perfect backdrop for the 24-hour Canary Coffee Shop which serves varied buffets and offers an à la carte menu and Theme Nights to the accompaniment of a resident band.

Above the marbled lobby are the hotel's 390 de luxe rooms and suites overlooking the Gulf

The 24-hour Canary Coffee Shop sports a romantic setting.

waters. Each room features 24-hour room service, extra large beds, individually-controlled air-conditioning, a well-stocked mini fridge, direct-dial telephone, television and in-house video.

Among the variety of dining outlets, the Oriental Restaurant serves specialities from China, Thailand, Arabia, India and the Philippines.

The pillarless Mubarakia Ballroom is a popular venue for weddings and can accommodate a thousand people. Dinner arrangements for 350 people can be organised or a reception for up to 700 people. The Al Majlis Room on the 15th floor has a private balcony. Dinners for 80 people can easily be arranged here and together with the Al Yamama Room is ideal for select private parties and business meetings. Fully equipped conference facilities are available on request.

The theatre-style Nawaris, located on the ground floor, is suitable for 120 people or a children's party; the Auditorium can seat 300 people. Besides these, there are a selection of shops and salons the guests can visit.

The sandy private beach is a favourite haunt of guests and they can indulge in the host of sports activities the hotel provides. These include water-skiing, windsurfing, sailing, tennis and squash. Guests can avail themselves of the Health Club which offers a gymnasium, aerobics classes, steam and sauna baths and massage. The Continental Bowling Centre provides a six-lane bowling alley. There are also two swimming pools, one of which is heated.

The pillarless Mubarakia Ballroom can accommodate a thousand people.

De luxe rooms and suites overlook the Gulf waters.

Café La Fontaine offers a popular, casual atmosphere.

Relax at the La Bamba Beach Restaurant.

Sharjah Grand Hotel

An aura of elegance, luxury and warm hospitality is what one is surrounded with inside the Sharjah Grand Hotel. Gracious decor, with beautifully appointed furnishings compose the setting for the haute cuisine and impeccable service. Conveniently located not far from the airports of Dubai and Sharjah, the hotel is ideally suited for the business traveller and holiday-maker alike. It stands on one of Sharjah's most beautiful beaches, lapped by the warm waters of the Gulf.

Spacious and tastefully furnished, the 220 guest rooms offer a beautiful view of the Arabian Gulf. The soothing colour schemes enhance the comfort of the rooms which are centrally air-conditioned. Each one is equipped with an independent telephone and modern amenities including a mini bar, radio and colour television, featuring in-house movies to complement local programmes. The hotel also has an efficient laundry and dry cleaning facility and 24-hour room service.

The Sharjah Grand offers an exciting variety of dining outlets. The informal La Brasserie Restau-

The Sharjah Grand Hotel stands on one of Sharjah's most beautiful beaches.

The Grand Hall is ideal for ceremonies and weddings.

rant boasts a lavish à la carte menu and a daily gourmet luncheon buffet. A range of Theme Nights attracts guests throughout the week.

Set against lush greenery and fountains, Café La Fontaine is the place to relax over hot beverages or a light snack. Also available is a tempting selection of waffles, crêpes and refreshing ice cream concoctions. Sample continental delicacies or treat yourself to a gourmet buffet at L'Aquarium Coffee Shop.

The Konigs Klub is a lively discotheque with a genuine Bavarian atmosphere. And the hotel also handles outside catering to bring in the professional touch within the comfort of your own home. The staff will help you select a menu that suits your taste and budget.

Venues for business conferences, social events and entertainment programmes are well equipped in the hotel. La Belle Époque with a capacity of up to 200 seated guests not only serves a memorable range of international cuisine but provides an elegant and sophisticated setting for seminars, receptions and private functions. A special entertainment programme for children is provided on request.

The rooms sport soothing colour schemes.

The Grand Hall which can accommodate 800 seated guests and up to 1,000 at standing receptions, is ideal for ceremonies and weddings.

Soak up the sun on the hotel's exclusive beach-front or take a dip in the temperature-controlled swimming pool. Tantalise the taste buds with succulent barbequed meats and refreshing cocktails at the Beach Restaurant. If you've had your fill of relaxing and want a bit of activity, sports facilities include windsurfing, basket ball and table tennis. Tennis clinics are also held for adults and children on the hotel's courts.

ACKNOWLEDGEMENTS

I should like to thank United Colour Film Est. Professional Division for the provision and careful processing of the films used in this book, Maps Geosystems for providing the superb aerial photos, Marwan Khoury for generously lending me his car for my photography, and Roohi Ali Khan of Motivate Publishing for her editorial assistance.

I should also like to thank all those businessmen and officials in Sharjah who kindly gave their time to talk to me, and most especially Abdul Rahman Hassan of the Department of Information for his unfailing patience and helpfulness.

Above all, I wish to express my gratitude to HH Dr Sheikh Sultan bin Mohammed Al Qasimi, and the Government of Sharjah, whose support and sponsorship have made possible the publication of this book.

BIBLIOGRAPHY

Al Qasimi, Sultan M: *The Myth of Arab Piracy in the Gulf*, 1986.

Amiri Court, Press Affairs Directorate: *Sharjah in Fifteen Years Time 1974-1988*, 1990.

Boucharlat, Remy (ed): *Archaeological Surveys and Excavations in the Sharjah Emirate*, 1985 ff.

Buckingham, J S: *Travels in Assyria, Media and Persia*, 1829.

Centre for Documentation and Research, Abu Dhabi, for Arabic, American, Dutch, English and Portuguese documents.

de Albuquerque, A: *The Commentaries*, 1557; trans 1875.

Groom, Nigel: "Eastern Arabia in Ptolemy's Map', in *Proceedings of the Seminar for Arabian Studies*, 1986.

Hawley, Donald: *The Trucial States*, 1970.

Heard-Bey, Frauke: *From Trucial States to United Arab Emirates*, 1982.

Ibn Majid, Ahmed (trans. Ferrand G): *Instructions nautiques arabes et portugais*, 1928.

Lorimer J G: *Gazetteer of the Persian Gulf*, 1915.

Moser, Rene: *Welcome to Sharjah*, 1974.

Sharjah Chamber of Commerce: *Made in Sharjah*

Tomkinson, Michael: *The United Arab Emirates, an Insight and a Guide*, 1975.

Zahlan, Rosemarie Said: *The Origins of the United Arab Emirates*, 1978.

AUTHOR

Shirley Kay and her husband, the former British Consul General in Dubai, first came to the Middle East in 1965 and brought up their family of four children here. They visited the Emirates in 1968 and lived here for part of 1969, often travelling to Sharjah from Dubai.

Memories of that time include visits to the beautiful beaches of Al Khan and Hamriya with her children, wandering through the palm groves of Dhaid and watching bats emerge from the falaj at twilight. She also attended a ceremonial marchpast at the old airport, close to where the King Faisal Mosque now stands.

They came back to live in the Emirates from 1985 to 1990, and now make frequent return visits for both work and pleasure.

Shirley Kay has studied languages at Cambridge University, Arabic at Shemlan in the Lebanon, and Middle Eastern archaeology at the Institute of Archaeology in London.

The author of a dozen previous books on Middle Eastern countries, this is Shirley Kay's seventh book in the Arabian Heritage Series. She has also made some thirty documentary films of the area for Dubai Television.

INDEX

Bold type indicates picture

OTHER ARABIAN HERITAGE TITLES

Arabian Profiles
edited by Ian Fairservice
and Chuck Grieve

Land of the Emirates
by Shirley Kay

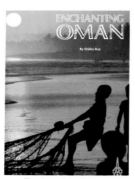
Enchanting Oman
by Shirley Kay

A Day Above Oman
by John Nowell

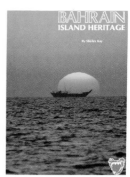
Bahrain-Island Heritage
by Shirley Kay

Dubai-Gateway to the Gulf
edited by Ian Fairservice

**Abu Dhabi-Garden City
of the Gulf** edited by Ian
Fairservice and Peter Hellyer

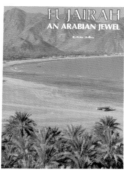
Fujairah-An Arabian Jewel
by Peter Hellyer

Portrait of Ras Al Khaimah
by Shirley Kay

**Architectural Heritage of
the Gulf** by Shirley Kay
and Dariush Zandi

**Emirates Archaeological
Heritage**
by Shirley Kay

**Mammals of the Southern
Gulf** by Christian Gross

The Living Desert
by Marycke Jongbloed

**Seashells of Southern
Arabia**
by Donald and Eloise Bosch

The Living Seas
by Frances Dipper and
Tony Woodward

Sketchbook Arabia
by Margaret Henderson

The Thesiger Collection —
a catalogue of unique
photographs by W Thesiger

**Juha-Last of the Errant
Knights** by Mustapha Kamal,
translated by Jack Briggs

**Snorkelling
and Diving
in Oman**
by
Rod Salm
and
Robert
Baldwin

**Off-Road
in the
Emirates**
by
Dariush
Zandi

**The Green
Guide to
the Emirates**
by
Marycke
Jongbloed

**Off-Road
in Oman**
by
Heiner Klein
and
Rebecca
Brickson